trotman

Get the Job You Want

10 Secrets to a Successful Job Search

Todd Bermont

Get the Job You Want
10 Secrets to a Successful Job Search

First published in the United States as *10 Insider Secrets to a Winning Job Search* by Careers Press, Inc, in 2004.
First published in Great Britain in 2009 by Trotman Publishing, an imprint of Crimson Publishing, Westminster House, Kew Road, Richmond, Surrey TW9 2ND.

Copyright © 2004, 2009 by Todd Bermont

Author: Todd Bermont

ISBN: 978 1 84455 215 3

British Library Cataloguing in Publication Data
A catalogue record for this book is available from the British Library.

Typeset by Cambridge Publishing Management Ltd
Printed and bound in Great Britain by MPG Books Ltd, Bodmin

Dedication

To my mother, Margot Bermont, my wife, Paula, and to my wonderful family and friends. Their tremendous love and support has given me the courage to follow a dream. I will always remember the advice my mother gave me in her final days:

> 'I would rather regret what I did do than
> what I didn't do!'

Living by those words has changed my life.

Contents

About the Author

Todd Bermont is president and founder of 10 Step Corporation, a firm specialising in sales training, sales consulting, keynote speaking and career coaching. Todd Bermont graduated with Honours from the University of Illinois. He has been a frequent guest lecturer at the University of Chicago and has taught job hunting online through many colleges and universities across the United States including the University of Wisconsin. Todd Bermont has been awarded the 'Certificate of Merit' by *Writer's Digest* magazine and 'Businessman of the Year' by the Business Advisory Council. Todd Bermont has also received numerous other sales and management awards throughout his career and has appeared several times on radio and television, and in national newspapers.

Having been a recruiting manager as well as an expert in sales, Todd Bermont brings a unique perspective to job hunting. Even today, as an author and speaker, Bermont uses the tips and techniques shared in this book. He is truly one author who 'walks the walk'. Prior to founding 10 Step Corporation, Bermont worked in executive management and corporate sales at some of the world's leading corporations, including Royal Dutch Shell, NCR, IBM and American Power Conversion.

Todd Bermont has worked in more than 20 countries, with more than half of the Fortune 500. As part of his goal to give back to the community, Bermont has also volunteered some of his time teaching job-hunting skills to inner-city secondary school students and to underprivileged individuals. Throughout his career, Bermont has helped thousands of people, across the globe, to succeed. Today, Todd Bermont is an internationally renowned author, professional speaker, sales trainer, executive career coach and consultant. You can find out more about Todd Bermont by visiting www.10stepjobsearch.com.

Acknowledgements

I am deeply grateful to everyone who has helped me in the preparation of this book. Thank you to Caryn Cialkowski, Harold Bermont, Sharon Maslov, Cheryl Southern, Debra Golden, Jennifer Fischer, Jeff Meyer and a special thank you to my wife, Paula. Also, thank you to the following individuals for your tremendous support and encouragement: Andrew Pultman, Nathaniel Bermont, Eric Bermont and Debbie Bermont. In addition, I would like to thank the 3rd Coast Café of Chicago for their endless cups of delicious coffee that helped keep me at the top of my game while writing this book.

I would also like to thank my previous employers for providing me with an outstanding foundation for my success: Royal Dutch Shell Corporation, NCR Corporation, IBM Corporation and American Power Conversion Corporation. Most importantly, I would like to thank each of you, the readers, for your confidence in me, in this book and in your own ability to succeed. In purchasing this book, you have invested your valuable time and money in what I have to say. I hope to exceed your expectations and help you land the job you want as quickly as possible.

Author's Note

Welcome to *Get the Job You Want*. Since coming out with my first book, *10 Insider Secrets to Job Hunting Success*, I have had the privilege of coaching clients, speaking in front of numerous groups and appearing live on both radio and television (including CNN and FOX), and have been featured in countless newspapers throughout the US, including the US edition of *CareerBuilder*.

As a result, I had the opportunity to talk to and gain feedback from thousands of people just like you. Even though my first book was often ranked the No. 1 'most popular' job-hunting book on sites such as Amazon.com and BN.com (Barnes & Noble), being a perfectionist, I wanted to add new and exciting topics and perspectives to make this book the best job-hunting resource ever created.

All the information contained in this book is based on my real-life job recruiting, job hunting, job interviewing, speaking and training experiences. My goal in writing this book is to provide you with the best possible foundation you need to get the job you want fast – even in difficult times.

This book is written to give you a complete step-by-step guide on how to get a job in any economy. It is my intention to offer you an entirely new perspective on job hunting that comes from both sides of the interview desk. *Get the Job You Want* is designed to provide you with an unfair advantage when searching for a job, and to help you have fun with the process. It is my sincerest hope that the secrets, strategies, tips and techniques you find here are beneficial not only in your job hunt, but also in your personal life.

With that being said, I would like to thank you for investing your valuable time and money in this book. I hope that you will be thrilled with your investment. Please enjoy!

Todd L. Bermont

Introduction

Congratulations! You have taken an important step towards having a successful job search and getting the job you have always wanted. This book is written to give you an unfair advantage. Once you've read it you'll feel confident and enthusiastic about yourself and the job hunt and, more importantly, you'll interview to win – so that you can get the job you want, at a salary you desire.

The Secrets In This Book Work!

Using these secrets, I have found jobs in both good times and bad, landed three job offers in one week (during a recession), earned numerous job promotions and received six job offers in my final year of university. You, too, can achieve this kind of success if you follow the tips and techniques in this book. Whether you want a position in a large corporation or a small entrepreneurial firm, after reading this book, you will jump into the job hunt like a champion and interview to win.

It Takes 24 Hours To Get The Ball Rolling!

This book teaches you everything you need to know to get the job you want – and how to sell yourself throughout the process. It is a complete job-hunting roadmap. The directions are logical, easy to follow and designed to show you exactly how to get your ideal job fast.

If you spend 24 solid hours following the advice in this book, you will have the foundation you need to succeed, even in today's job market.

With this book, you will:
- Maintain a winning attitude throughout your job search
- Discover the job you really want
- Convince firms to employ you even when no positions are open
- Write attention-grabbing CVs and covering letters

- Network and market yourself to maximise your job opportunities
- Be prepared for even the most rigorous job interviews
- Answer the most difficult interview questions
- Interview to win even on the toughest job interviews
- Learn how to negotiate your job offers to receive top whack.

I'll Share Real-Life Experience . . .
From Both Sides Of The Interviewing Desk

The secrets in this book are based on my experience both as a job hunter as well as a job interviewer. I have been in your shoes. I understand the frustrations and challenges that can often accompany a job search and I know how to overcome them. As a recruitment manager, I have also been in the interviewer's shoes. I will share with you their perspectives and how to use that information to your advantage.

While today I may be a 'job-hunting expert', it certainly wasn't always that way. In fact, there have been many times when I have flat out failed in my pursuit of the ideal job. Even now, when I forget to embrace one or more of the secrets in this book, I can still be humbled. However, having learned the secrets in this book, I no longer fear interviews, doubt myself or get frustrated at circumstances. Instead, I approach every opportunity with confidence and excitement. Now, I have the career of my dreams and I am happier than ever.

If I Can Do It, You Can Too!

As an author and professional speaker, even to this day, I still have to job hunt on a daily basis. The only difference is now I interview for jobs that last anywhere from five minutes to several days, instead of finding an opportunity that will last for years. To appear on radio or TV, I have to go through the same kinds of gruelling interviews that you do. Whenever a corporation or university considers hiring me to speak, they put me through the wringer. On average, to make a media appearance or to win a speaking engagement, I have to go through at least three to four job interviews. In this book, I'll share with you the same tips and techniques I use in my own job searches.

Certainly, the job-hunting process is a lot easier for me now than it was years ago. After all, I have gone through hundreds of interviews, been hired many times, and I have had the good fortune of sitting on the other side of the interviewing desk as a recruitment manager. However, I am far from perfect. What I can tell you is that when I follow the secrets in this book, typically I succeed. It's when I get too cocky, and forget one or two of them, that I get slapped back into reality.

I once lost the opportunity of a lifetime

The opportunity was with Procter & Gamble. For years I had wanted to work for them. Finally, I was granted an interview. To me, this job opportunity was the chance of a lifetime. I was both eager and nervous at the same time. Unfortunately, while I was extremely excited about the opportunity, I wasn't nearly as prepared for what I was about to encounter. All of a sudden, as I was walking to the interview, my knees started to buckle and my legs began to quiver. Then, my hands started to sweat more than the outside of an air conditioner on a hot day. No matter how many times I wiped my hands on my suit trousers, they still were dripping wet. I kept telling myself to relax. But the more I told myself that, the more nervous I got.

When I got to the interview, there was not just one person interviewing me, but two. When I shook their hands, they must have thought they were shaking a cold fish. They told me to take a seat. I almost missed the chair as I went to sit down. That's when things went from bad to worse. First, I was asked to tell them about myself. I didn't know where to start. I rambled and rambled and finally stopped when I saw one of the interviewers staring out of the window in complete boredom. Then, they asked me what my biggest challenge was and how I overcame it. I had no clue. Has your mind ever gone completely blank? Well, that's what happened to me.

The interview went so badly that, to save face at the end, I actually said to the interviewers, 'I greatly appreciate your time today. However, after learning more about the position, I have to say that I don't think this is the right job for me.' Afterwards, I was devastated. Here, I was interviewing with a company for which I had always wanted to work and I totally blew it! It didn't matter that I got the last word, I just lost a dream job opportunity.

I was determined to succeed

After failing, I decided never again would I bungle an interview so badly. Never again would I go into an interview so unprepared. Never again would I be so nervous that my legs would tremble or my hands would drip with sweat. No! From that point on, I have been determined to succeed and, fortunately, have been able to enjoy many great achievements.

How I Did It

Getting the Job You Want is the culmination of what I have learned over the years to be the foundation for success. You could read nine separate books on careers, covering letters, job interviewing, job hunting, motivation, negotiating, networking, CVs and selling and still not get the information you'll discover in this book.

Throughout this book, you'll see many references to the art of selling. The reason is plain and simple. In order for you to get a job, you have to sell yourself throughout the entire job-hunting process. The interesting thing about job hunting is, while you are the salesperson, you are also the product. This book will help you balance both roles to get the sale – a great job offer!

Gain Confidence And Achieve Success!

You'll feel so confident in yourself, and have such a good game plan for your search, that you'll actually look forward to job hunting. You'll even realise that you can really enjoy the interviewing process. In the end, you will succeed.

You'll Get The Job You Have Always Wanted!

My ultimate goal for this book is for you to get the job you want, at a salary you desire, as quickly as possible. With that being said, I would like once again to thank you for investing your valuable time and money in this book. Please enjoy!

Secret No. 1

Believe in Yourself

- 10 ways to develop and maintain a positive attitude throughout your job search.

The most basic, yet perhaps the most essential, secret to any successful job search is to believe in yourself and your ability to succeed. After all, if you don't believe in yourself, who will? Optimism fosters clear thought, energy, enthusiasm and productivity. When you believe that you are a great person you can achieve great things. Whether dating, investing, playing sports or job hunting, it's much easier to succeed when you are confident and happy than when you are down and depressed. When you feel positive about yourself and your situation, it is easier to enjoy all that life has to offer – including job hunting!

Developing and maintaining a positive attitude is an essential ingredient to any successful job search. I will now take you through 10 ways that, in as little as 30 seconds or less, can help you develop and maintain a positive mental attitude throughout your job hunt.

---

10 ways to develop and maintain a positive attitude

1 Believe that 'you are great'.
2 Understand that everything happens for a reason.
3 Get some R, R and R (rest, relaxation and reflection).
4 Tell yourself 'I can do it!'
5 Think of interviewing as a numbers game.
6 Surround yourself with positive people.
7 Don't take rejection personally.
8 Treat interviewing like a job.
9 Focus on what you can control.
10 Visualise success.

---

1. Believe That 'You Are Great'

Wait! You're wondering whether or not you're a great person?
Stop right there. Every person, in his or her own way, is great.
You don't believe me? Well, start believing! If you don't believe
in yourself and your abilities how can you expect others to believe
in you? If you lack confidence because you feel others are more
qualified, forget it!

The word 'qualified' is subjective

You don't need DEFRA to place a big, blue 'Interview Approved'
stamp on your forehead. Being qualified is totally subjective. The key
is to position yourself so you become qualified. Don't worry. By the
time you finish this book, you will be able to present your qualities and
characteristics so no one can defeat you. Remember Tony the Tiger
from the Kellogg's Frosties adverts and how he used to say, 'They're
grrreeeeaaaaat!' If you want to feel good, just look at yourself in a
mirror and smile. Then, like Tony the Tiger, yell out as loud as you
can, 'I am grrreeeeaaaaat!' Say it with conviction. I know it sounds
silly, but try it. I guarantee you will have a smile on your face. Say it
often enough and you will believe it. You are great! Don't let anyone
tell you otherwise!

Still down? Try creating a list of your accomplishments

If you are still having difficulty believing in yourself, take out a sheet
of paper and write down as many of your accomplishments as you
possibly can. Write down anything that comes to mind. And don't
worry about staying focused on just work-related accomplishments.
Your accomplishments can be something as simple as scoring a goal
in a soccer game, getting a good mark in a difficult assignment,
successfully leading a group project, winning a major sale, or solving
a difficult customer situation. Be it in our relationships, our family
life, in school or in our careers, we have all had numerous
accomplishments throughout our lives. By taking the time to write
down some of your many accomplishments you begin to realise that
you truly are a great person.

2. Understand That Everything Happens For A Reason

Right now, many of you may be experiencing difficult times. Perhaps that's why you purchased this book. But don't feel sorry for yourself or make excuses for your situation. These feelings will only sabotage your efforts. One of my friends recently lost his job, even though he was working more than 14 hours a day. He was devastated when the company decided to let him go. He had worked as hard as humanly possible and had to travel almost all the time. On top of that, he was a top producer. Yet, in the end, what was his reward? A P45! In fact, he even had to take legal action against the company just to recoup what he was owed in bonus money.

I had a long conversation with him. I said, 'You know what? This is the best thing that could have happened to you.' At first, he thought I was crazy. How could losing a job possibly be good?

I said to him, 'You have had no life. Your entire life was the company. Look at you. You don't have a relationship. Your health is not good. You're constantly going to the doctor. And let's face it, when was the last time you took a holiday where you relaxed and didn't check voice mail and email every day?'

He started to smile. 'You are right,' he said. Even though he had been making more money than ever, he wasn't happy because he had no balance in his life. With his new perspective, he suddenly realised losing his job was an opportunity to regain his life, health and balance, not a failure as he had originally thought. He was now free to find a new job that would allow him everything he truly wanted in life.

Sometimes it takes a tremendous amount of pain to force us to make changes for the better. Think about it, when you are complacent with something in your life, do you go through the effort to change it?

It can even take losing a job to provide the incentive to find a much better position.

If you were laid off or fired . . .

This is an opportunity, not a hurdle. Be proud of who you are and what you have accomplished in your life. As with my friend, everything happens for a reason.

You may not know what that reason is today. However, in five years, you will look back on this time and be glad you went through this discovery process. This is the universe's way of saying it is time to take a time-out and improve your situation. After all, you deserve better!

Tell yourself that you lost your job so you can finally be free to find the job of your dreams or to regain balance in your life. Every person I know who has lost his or her job ultimately ended up in a much better situation. You will too! You deserve a better situation and you will find it.

If you are graduating or are currently employed ...

This is okay. You just haven't found the right opportunity yet. Be full of pride. Celebrate your successes and accomplishments. Believe that you are an extraordinary person and you will get the job you want. If you were rejected at some interviews, it is only because there is something better for you elsewhere.

Not all opportunities will be right for you

I can tell you firsthand that even I get rejected on interviews from time to time. You might think, 'wait a minute, you're the author of a job-hunting book, why do you even go on interviews, let alone experience rejection? I thought you knew it all.'

Well, as an author and a speaker, I am constantly being interviewed for speaking engagements and radio and television appearances. Just like you, I have to sell myself to win each and every opportunity. I can totally relate to what you are going through. Although I am an 'expert' on the topic, sometimes even I don't succeed.

Whenever I get rejected, I try to take a step back and recap the situation. I try to see what I can learn from an interview so I don't repeat the same mistakes again. Then, I think to myself, there was a reason why I didn't succeed on this interview. I try to work out what that reason was and then I tell myself it just wasn't the right opportunity for me.

By realising that everything happens for a reason, you can take solace in knowing that no matter what challenges are thrown your way, ultimately you will be in a much better situation to succeed. Every step you take is getting you that much closer to happiness and success.

3. Get Some R, R And R (Rest, Relaxation And Reflection)

Before starting any job hunt, it is critical to have as much energy and enthusiasm as possible. Whether you have lost your job, or you just want to find something better, I always recommend taking some time off to rest, relax and reflect. One of the best ways I have found to re-energise myself is to do something outdoors. Be it a walk on the beach, a hike, a bicycle ride or going to the pond to watch the ducks, I have found that doing something outdoors does a world of good for my mental state of being. It helps me temporarily escape my daily problems and, best of all, it is free!

Personally, I love taking long walks to reflect on my current situation. It is amazing the ideas I can get as a result of just taking a walk. Like you, there are times when I can get disgusted over a situation or an outcome. To overcome this frustration, I try to dissect the situation by asking myself questions such as 'Why did this happen? What can I learn? How could I have done it differently? Where did I do well and how can I improve? How will going through this make me a better person?' By answering these questions, I always end up feeling better.

Don't be afraid to be honest with yourself

If you lost your job or if you are unhappy in your current career, try to understand why. Be objective with yourself. Sometimes the truth hurts. However, it's better you learn now, so you can avoid similar situations and outcomes in the future. There once was a time when I was a manager for American Power Conversion (APC) where I almost got fired. This was my first job as a manager. I was so focused on wanting to impress upper management that I was totally failing in my management duties. Luckily, my boss at the time suggested I ask my employees to conduct a review of me. When I did this, I was shocked at the comments they made about me.

They wrote statements such as 'Didn't go to bat for us' and 'Doesn't listen to our needs'. Until I went through this process, I had no idea that I had become the type of boss for whom I myself had always hated to work. Fortunately, I had the opportunity to learn from my mistakes and correct them before I got fired. From then I have always had my employees review me. Thankfully, the reviews have always been better ever since. However, not everyone is fortunate enough to be given a second opportunity to learn before losing a job. If you fail in this category, or if you just are flat miserable on your current job, ask yourself some tough questions that will help you move on to success.

Ask yourself questions such as, 'Where can I make improvements? What do I really want in an ideal job? Where do I want to focus my energies? What can I do differently in the future to have a better outcome?'

Look past the negatives and see all of the positives you have experienced throughout your career. Summarise your learning experiences. Ask yourself what you liked most and what you liked least about your last position. This will help you focus your job hunt.

Ideally you want to find a job that maximises the things you like most and minimises those you like least. While this is such a simple concept, people often fail to take into account their true likes and dislikes. Then they wonder why they end up switching jobs or getting fired every two to three years.

By taking the time to rest, relax and reflect, you get a better perspective on your current situation and gain the energy you need to succeed. You can then jump into your job hunt with the excitement of a lion being fed a nice juicy steak.

4. Tell Yourself 'I Can Do It!'

Keep your spirits up! A great way to feel confident at any time is to yell out with joy and confidence 'I can do it!' Remember when John Belushi shouted out 'Let's do it!' in the film *Animal House*? Try going to a mirror and scream like John Belushi 'I can do it!' Then yell out 'I will get the job I want!' When you shout with conviction 'I can do it! I will get the job I want!' you will believe it.

Have you ever noticed how it's the positive people who always seem to be the happiest and most successful? Upbeat people are fun to be around. They are also the ones who tend to get the most out of life. A positive attitude is contagious. Those who catch it are for ever cured.

You can do it! You will get the job of your dreams!

5. Think Of Interviewing As A Numbers Game

At times, your job hunt may become frustrating, especially if you experience rejection. However, don't let it get you down or strip away your confidence. Depending on the job you are trying to get, it may take as many as 10 interviews just to get one offer. But by reading this book, you are increasing your chances for success. Look at each rejection as bringing you one interview closer to getting the job you really want. If you get rejected after an interview, say to yourself, 'This job wasn't a good fit. I deserve better. I am too good for them. Besides, I am one interview closer to getting the job I really want!'

Don't get emotionally attached to any single opportunity. Focus on the process and what you can learn from each situation. If you get rejected, try to understand why. In fact, there is absolutely nothing wrong with calling an interviewer and asking why you didn't get the offer. After all, you invested valuable time and energy preparing for and going on the interview. You have a right to know.

Not every position will be the right job for you. Interviewing is a numbers game. Each rejection serves as an opportunity to improve, as well as a stepping stone that gets you that much closer to your ideal job.

6. Surround Yourself With Positive People

When going through an arduous job hunt, it is easy to be sidetracked by negative thoughts and pessimistic people. But to succeed you must avoid these damaging elements as much as possible. Dwelling on the negative will only hurt your efforts. Instead, focus on the positives. Surround yourself with people who will encourage you and motivate you. When you are around positive people you'll think and perform like a winner.

Job hunting is like the property business

They say it is always better to buy the cheapest house in a good neighbourhood than to buy the most expensive house in a questionable area. The value of the lowest priced house in a good neighbourhood is almost always boosted by the presence of the more expensive houses.

When you surround yourself with positive and motivating people, like a good neighbourhood, their enriching attitudes will rub off on you and boost your morale, success and overall value. These positive influences can only help you succeed.

If you have negative friends, stay away from them while you're job hunting. If members of your family are negative, tell them to keep their thoughts to themselves unless they have something constructive to say. I know this can be difficult, especially when dealing with family, but attitude is so important!

Attitude can often determine success or failure

Like it or not, each one of us emits energy, be it positive energy or negative. Subconsciously, we tune into the frequencies of others. Don't make the mistake of spending most of your time commiserating with people who are frustrated and out of work. You'll soak up their negative energy like a dry sponge. Instead, surround yourself with positive people who are succeeding in what they do.

Employed and happy people are much more likely to help you succeed than those who are negative and unemployed. So, be positive, confident and surround yourself with motivating people who will help you succeed.

7. Don't Take Rejection Personally

One of the most difficult tasks of any job hunt is to not take rejection personally. However, in job hunting, there are many things that are beyond your control. Just understand that this process is the universe's gift to help you find a much more fulfilling opportunity. Rarely in life does something worthwhile ever come easily. Each bump in the road is a step on your stairway to success. If an interviewer wants to employ an Oxford graduate and you went to Sussex, there is nothing you can do to change it. Not every situation will be the right one for you. If the only thing the interviewer was interested in was where you went to university or college, then you probably wouldn't want to work for them anyway. Don't take it personally. Rejection is just a part of the job-hunting process.

8. Treat Interviewing Like A Job

Typically, the people who have the greatest success at job hunting are those who treat the job hunt like a job in itself. This attitude fosters motivation and productivity. After all, getting a new job is a job in itself. Anyone who tells you otherwise is mistaken. There are many steps you can take to treat your job hunt like a job – and put yourself in a position to succeed.

Dress the part every day

If you are trying to get a job that requires formal business attire, then wear something professional every day. When you dress the part, you live it and feel it. You never know whether, during the course of any given day, you might run into someone who can employ you. I have known of people who found jobs just by talking to complete strangers while in airports, bus stations, local coffee shops or even on a commuter train. If an opportunity presents itself, you want to be at your very best.

When you dress for success, you achieve it. Even if you have a phone interview, dress as if you were interviewing in person. When you dress the part, you will communicate much more effectively and you put yourself in a much better frame of mind to succeed.

Believe it or not, the person you are talking to can subconsciously sense how you are dressed, even over the phone. If the job you are striving for requires business casual attire, rather than formal, then wear that every day. The key is to dress how you would dress if you were on the job. Doing so energetically puts you in the proper frame of mind.

Establish a virtual office

Another way to treat the job hunt like a job is to go to a 'virtual' office every day. The secret is to go somewhere. Some of my clients have gone to places such as the library, while others have gone to a coffee shop or a bookstore café. Some have even gone to the extent of renting an executive office suite. Others have found friends who could lend them a spare desk where they work.

Look for a place that is within your budget. Yet find a location where you can be productive. When you get out of the house, you feel better about yourself. You also avoid distractions such as the television, the internet, children and housework. Ultimately, you become much more productive, confident and proud.

Get a new email address

In today's day and age, almost everyone is connected to the internet. Most companies prefer to communicate electronically. Having a professional email address allows you to level the playing field. I suggest you create a new address just for your job search. That way your job-hunting related emails won't get confused with junk mail and other mail that is less important. Also, new accounts are much less likely to receive annoying spam.

When you are creating your account, make it as professional as possible. Don't use anything silly such as a nickname, a number or a catchy phrase. Instead, try to use your first initial and your last name. That way, interviewers will recognise your incoming emails. If the ideal email ID isn't available, then try your full name. Everything you do conveys an image. Something as minute as your email address can make or break someone's impression of you.

If you don't have your own computer . . .

With today's technology, there are many ways you can establish an email account without having your own computer. Sites such as Hotmail.com, btinternet.com and Yahoo.com provide this service either free or for a nominal fee. These sites store your email online so you can access it from any computer. You can go to a local internet café to get on a computer, or just ask a friend if you can use theirs.

Have a personal business card

When you have a personal business card you convey a more positive and professional image. Also, most people feel more important and confident when they have a business card. Perhaps best of all, business cards are especially convenient to use when networking.

Creating a business card is easy

There are numerous software solutions you can use to design a business card. In fact, many PCs even provide templates. Business cards are very inexpensive to produce. Typically, you can print out 500 for the cost of eating a meal in a restaurant. Either you can buy business card stock paper for your computer printer or you can take your file to a local printer or copy shop. If you don't have a computer, most printing companies and copy shops can assist you in creating a professional card. Either route you choose, the cost of producing a professional business card is relatively inexpensive and well worth the investment.

Make your business card simple, yet professional
If you are not sure what it should look like, go into your drawer or filing cabinet and take out a handful of old business cards you have collected throughout the years. If you don't have any, then call up a friend and ask to see some of theirs.

Include a logo or picture
For your logo, you can use your initials in a bigger and different font or you can insert a picture of yourself. I know, I know, people have always said that you don't want to put a picture on anything when job hunting. However, my feeling is that if you want to, then go right ahead. Let's face it, if someone is going to reject you on the basis of your appearance, isn't it better not to waste the time and energy on the interview? Having a picture on your card can help interviewers put a face to your name. However, do what is most comfortable for you.

Give yourself a title
For a title, put whatever the position is that you are trying to get. If you want to get an accounting position, then put 'accountant'.

If you want a sales position, then put something like 'sales representative' or 'account manager'. Or just put your name on the card without a title.

Provide important contact information
Include your address, phone number and email address. Since much business is now conducted globally, it's important to give the international prefix when you give your phone number. For a UK number, for example, the number should be given in the following way: +44 (0)123 456789. Provide information that makes you most accessible. If you have a mobile phone, you may want to use that instead of your home phone. Most software packages have a variety of templates and fonts you can use.

TLB   **Todd L. Bermont**

1 Main Street   Tel: +44 (0)123 456789
Jobville AB12 3CD   tbermont@10stepjobsearch.com

Use voicemail

One of my biggest 'pet peeves' when I have interviewed people in the past, was when I called someone who either didn't have voicemail or didn't have a professional greeting. The worst messages are those that have loud music and you can't even hear what the message is saying.

Forget answering machines
Only voicemail can provide you with the professionalism that you need to succeed in today's competitive times. No, I don't work for your phone company. The bottom line is that if you don't have voicemail and you are on the phone, your interviewer will get a busy signal. This will happen regardless of whether or not you have a recording machine. And if you are not home, even with an

answering machine, your phone could ring endlessly. In either case, an interviewer may never call you again. Often, you only get one chance. Don't blow it with a cheap answering machine.

Voicemail is available from most phone companies including mobile phone providers. Typically, it is very inexpensive. If you don't have it, get it! Answering machines are just not professional or reliable.

Have a professional greeting

Interviewers don't want to hear rock music, a computer-generated voice or your children on your recorded message. They want to hear a professional greeting from you.

Your greeting is just one more way you can demonstrate the high-calibre individual that you are. Here is an example of a greeting I often use.

Sample voicemail message

Thank you for calling the voicemail box of Todd Bermont. I am currently away from my desk, but please leave your message after the tone and I will try to return your call within three business hours. Thank you.

Notice, I don't say I am *either* on the phone or away from my desk. I just say I am away from my desk. There is a reason for this. How is your interviewer supposed to know which one it is? If you aren't home, but the interviewer thinks you are on the phone, they may have an unrealistic expectation that you will get back to them quickly. It's better just to say you are 'away from the desk'. That way you can exceed the expectation, rather than risk falling short.

Dedicate the proper time and effort to your job hunt

If you were working at a full-time or part-time job, you would probably go to work every day and consistently show up on time. Searching for a job requires the same effort. To be successful, you must dedicate a certain amount of time solely to the purpose of the job hunt.

If you are unemployed: Dedicate a minimum of eight hours a day to your job-hunting activities. This can be spent in a variety of ways, from doing research, to networking, to improving your CV. Practice counts as well. Think about it: a football team will practise an entire week to play just one three-hour game. You need to put that kind of effort into your job search.

If you are employed or a student, devote at least two to three hours a day. If you cannot afford to do that, then schedule two or three days out of the week, when you can spend that amount of time. Treat job hunting, in this case, like a part-time job.

I understand you might think this is difficult. But if you don't take job hunting seriously, you will not get the job you want, in the timeframe you desire. After all, your competition is taking it very seriously! When you treat your job search like a job, you will have a higher self-esteem, be more productive and will convey a more positive image. Ultimately, treating your job hunt like a job will directly contribute to the success you achieve and the level of your morale throughout the process.

9. Focus On What You Can Control

In life, as well as in job hunting, there are many things we cannot control. We cannot control things such as the economy, politics, taxes and whether or not the country is at war. However, there are many things we can control. We can control aspects such as:

- Diet
- Exercise
- Attitude
- Organisation
- Focus.

When you focus on those things that you can control, somehow the things you cannot control become less cumbersome. I know when I eat right, exercise regularly, properly focus my energies, and organise, I have a much more positive attitude about myself. Additionally, I am much more productive.

Focusing on those areas you can control will help you immensely. It will give you a sense of accomplishment every day.

10. Visualise Success

Perhaps the best exercise of all is visualisation. When my mother was alive she used to always try to convince us kids, when we were down or scared about a situation, to visualise a good outcome. Being a typical child, her words usually went in one ear, and out the other. However, over the years, I have learned the value of her advice. I wish I had listened years ago. Visualisation really works.

Every morning when you wake up, take a few moments to close your eyes and visualise success. Visualise an interviewer reaching across the desk and shaking your hand, saying, 'Congratulations, welcome to our team.' Or, 'Congratulations . . . You're hired!' Before every interview, visualise the outcome you want. If it is a phone interview, visualise the interviewer asking you to come in for a second interview. If you are interviewing in person, visualise the interviewer offering you a job.

When you visualise success, you achieve it

Hopefully by now you are feeling better about yourself and your situation. When you believe in yourself, you can succeed at almost anything. Thomas Edison failed thousands of times before he finally found the solution to inventing the light bulb.

Colonel Harland Sanders, founder of Kentucky Fried Chicken, went to thousands of restaurants before he finally found someone willing to take a chance on his recipe for chicken. Both Thomas Edison and Colonel Sanders had one thing in common. They believed in themselves. If you believe, you will achieve! So before moving on to the next chapter, close your eyes and visualise success. You are great! You can do it! You will get the job you want at a salary you desire!

Checklist Summary

✓ Say out loud 'I'm great!'
✓ Everything happens for a reason.

✓ Get some rest, relaxation and reflection.
✓ Interviewing is just a numbers game.
✓ Surround yourself with positive people.
✓ Smile and shout 'I can do it!'
✓ Don't take rejection personally.
✓ Treat the job search like a job.
✓ Focus on what you can control.
✓ When you visualise success, you achieve it.

'A positive attitude is contagious. Those who catch it are
forever cured!'

Secret No. 2

Identify Your Core Strengths and Competencies

- The four cornerstones of strengths and competencies
- Convert strengths and competencies into benefits.

Losing a job or searching for a new position can be frustrating. It can be especially difficult if you have the pressures of unpaid bills, supporting loved ones or dealing with an unbearable boss. It can certainly be tempting to just jump into the job hunt and put the misery behind you or to just dive into the classified ads and post lots of CVs. However, before you do so, it is important to take a step back to assess your strengths, capabilities and talents. Then, determine what it is you really want to accomplish and do for a living.

Create A Solid Foundation

The best way to jump-start your job search is to first identify your core strengths and competencies – what you are good at. You will be amazed at how proud of yourself and more confident in your abilities and opportunities you become when you take the time to acknowledge your positives. These core strengths and competencies are the foundation on which your job hunt is built.

Insider Tip
During your interviews, more than 80% of the time you will be asked, 'What are some of your greatest strengths?' By articulating your strengths and competencies now, you will be much more prepared when asked this question in your next interview.

Knowing your strengths helps focus your job hunt

When you know what you are good at, it helps you focus your job hunt on those jobs you are most likely able to get. Unfortunately, even the best sometimes forget to do this. Have you ever heard of the basketball player Michael Jordan? After winning three championships in the early 1990s, he decided to retire from basketball to try baseball and golf. Because he was a tremendous athlete, Michael was confident he could succeed at these other sports, too. As it turned out, Michael didn't perform nearly as well in those sports as he did in basketball. Fortunately, he realised this and returned to basketball, where his talents were most aligned. He went on to win several more championships and to conquer many more milestones. Unless you have the financial resources of Michael Jordan, it is best to focus your job hunt on those positions in which you have a talent and expertise, and would best succeed.

Insider Tip

During your interviews, you will probably be asked, 'Why did you choose this occupation?' By articulating your strengths and competencies, you have a strong foundation on which to answer this question.

Separate yourself from the competition

As of yet, I am not aware of any human clones. One of the beauties of life is that we are all unique. Each of us has positives and negatives. I have yet to meet a perfect person, but I have yet to meet someone who doesn't have numerous redeeming factors. The key is to use your positives to your advantage.

In job interviewing, it is your core strengths and competencies, along with your personality and appearance, that ultimately differentiate you from your competition. Identifying your core strengths is like reading a fuel gauge in a car. When driving, the more fuel you have, the further you can travel. Similarly, the more skills and experience you have accumulated throughout your career, the further you can go in your work-related endeavours.

When you review your strengths, be honest with yourself. It will help you identify those positions you realistically can consider. For example, if you have just graduated from university or college, it would be pretty difficult to get a position as a head of department. However, if you have been in the workforce for many years and have significant management experience, perhaps the position is more realistic.

In your career, just as in driving, you can always put more fuel in your tank and travel further. The key is to determine your destination and draw a road map (plan) of how to get there. Each job you hold and degree you attain along the way, in conjunction with the knowledge and experience you gain, serves as more fuel for your career.

To see how far you can realistically travel at this point in your career, assess your core strengths and competencies. You will be able to identify the jobs that you want, as well as those that you have the best opportunity to get. Everyone has unique strengths. Identify yours so you can focus your efforts where you are most likely to be recruited.

Job interviewing is like dating

In dating, your appearance may be important to some people, while others might look for someone with a great personality. Some may want to date a person who comes from a good family background, while others may fancy a person with a good sense of humour and an appealing laugh.

Whether it's our personality, our looks, our smile or our sense of humour, we all have different strengths and attributes that make each of us attractive to someone else. The same is true in interviewing. Some interviewers look for candidates with a great personality or extensive work experience, while others may want someone with corporate expertise or who is a team player.

The key is to identify your greatest selling points so you can make yourself as appealing to your potential employers as possible. I know you have a tremendous ability to succeed. Be it in school, on the job, or in your personal life, I am confident you have developed many marketable strengths and competencies. Now is the time to articulate them.

I have never been in an interview situation without being asked the question, 'What are your strengths?' Because it is so common, you need to be prepared. There are four cornerstones you can use to articulate your strengths and competencies:

The four cornerstones of strengths and competencies

1 Personality and subconscious energy.
2 Personal and job-related accomplishments.
3 Work-related skills.
4 Job-related knowledge and credentials.

---

1. Personality And Subconscious Energy

Have you ever met someone on the street and immediately felt comfortable with that person? Conversely, has anyone ever rubbed you up the wrong way before you even had the chance to meet them? What causes this? Often it is their personality and the subconscious energy they emit.

Subconscious energy can be described as waves of power that cannot be seen, but can certainly be felt. Each of us, whether or not we choose to acknowledge it, is a transmitter of energy. How we feel about ourselves and our lives determines the frequency of energy that we release. People who are happy in life and proud of who they are have an unmistakable glow about them that can be understood, even without them talking. Conversely, those who are depressed and ashamed walk around with a 'cloud' over their head.

In job hunting, and in life in general, how you feel about yourself and your situation will absolutely determine the frequency of energy that you produce. That energy will significantly impact on the type of people you attract in your life and the quality of life that you live.

What level of energy are you broadcasting?

If you have gone from one bad job to another or one bad relationship to another, perhaps you should question the feelings you have about your life and about yourself. Your energy is like a radio. When you tune in to your favourite radio programme, you are tuning into a station that is transmitting at a particular frequency. Everyone else who tunes into that frequency will hear the same station.

In subconscious energy, when you are broadcasting depressed, frustrated and insecure waves, you will only attract others into your life who are tuned in to those same negative frequencies. On the other hand, if you make a conscious decision to be proud of yourself, and to cherish all the positive things you have in life, you'll attract people who are winners and who will want to help you in your pursuit of the ideal job.

'The energy you transmit will impact on your entire job search, from networking to job interviewing.'

Gratitude: the easiest way to establish positive energy

Gratitude is powerful. One of the best ways to change negative energy into positive is to focus on those things in life for which you are most thankful. Often in life we can take things for granted. Just being able to walk is something to be grateful for. How many people in the world are disabled and unable to simply walk up a flight of stairs?

If I fall into the trap of feeling sorry for myself, I place my emphasis on gratitude instead of frustration and disappointment, and it doesn't take long to snap out of the negative mood. In job hunting it's easy to fall into a trap of doom and gloom. After all, there are many others who are more than happy to join you in that trap. Instead, focus on all of the good things in your life.

Rather than focusing on your lack of a job, or a rejection you just encountered, think about positives such as having a family and good friends, having your health, having love in your life or having experienced wonderful things.

Try starting each day by focusing on gratitude
Get into the habit of articulating every morning at least five things in your life for which you are grateful. You can pick any five. Just be genuine in what you choose. When you start each day with gratitude, you'll tune into a positive frequency that'll attract success and happiness in your life and your job hunt. This certainly beats waking up 'on the

wrong side of the bed'. When I start my days thinking about the good in life, I almost always have a great day. When I forget to do this, it is amazing how many distractions, roadblocks, and frustrations pop up.

The conscious visualisation of subconscious energy

As previously mentioned, each of us, at all times, is broadcasting waves of energy that cannot be seen but are indeed felt by the subconscious mind. However, there is a conscious representation of this subconscious energy you transmit – your personality. While each job interviewer will have an immediate subconscious feeling about you, they will consciously relate to your personality.

Understanding and being able to articulate your personality will help you focus your job hunt and sell yourself during interviews. There are both general and work-related aspects to our personalities.

1   General personality traits provide insight into your overall personality, both inside and outside the workplace. Are you easy-going? Do you have an outgoing personality? Descriptions such as positive, creative, people-oriented, competitive, driven, empathetic, assertive, flexible and motivated are examples of your general personality strengths.

2   Work-related personality traits describe aspects of your personality that are more relevant to the workplace and on-the-job performance. Descriptions such as team-oriented, goal-oriented, strategic thinker, natural leader, conscientious, detail-oriented and problem-solver are examples of job-related personality strengths. If I asked you what your greatest personality traits were, what would you say?

Insider Tip
When interviewers say, 'Tell me about yourself', what they are really looking for are aspects of your personality, both general and work-related, and whether they make you the most viable candidate for the position.

2. Personal And Job-Related Accomplishments

Accomplishments are quantifiable results that you have achieved throughout your life and career. This second cornerstone provides an objective insight into your abilities and achievements. Interviewers often use accomplishments both as a way to differentiate one candidate from another and as a means to justify their decisions based on emotion. As we discussed on pages 24–6, energy cannot be seen; it is only felt. That energy often stimulates emotions, either in a positive or a negative way, within the interviewer. An interviewer may feel very enthusiastic about you without exactly knowing why, and to justify this excitement, he or she will often use your accomplishments as a means to logically explain his or her feelings.

Accomplishments generate interest throughout the job hunt

Because energy has no bounds, it flows into your CVs, into your covering letters and into your networking and interviews. This energy will always stimulate emotions within anyone encountered. As early as possible in your job-hunting process, you'll want to articulate your many accomplishments. You'll find that the more accomplishments you identify, building your confidence, the more positive your energy frequency will be. Once you have created a list of accomplishments, you can draw from it in everything from your CVs to your interviews. As with personality, there are two categories of accomplishments: personal and job-related.

1   Personal accomplishments summarise achievements of your life outside of work. Examples may include charitable activities, community service, offices held and sports championships.

2   Work-related accomplishments demonstrate successes you've had on the job. Achievements such as getting a great review, winning a company award, being featured in a corporate magazine, reducing expenses by 25% and receiving job promotions are all examples of job-related accomplishments. What accomplishments have you achieved? Focus on those accomplishments that are most applicable for the positions you are seeking and those that are most

quantifiable. Saying you reduced costs is a great accomplishment. But, what makes that accomplishment even stronger is if you can say you reduced costs by 15% resulting in savings of over £100,000. Now that's an accomplishment that will make an interviewer drool with excitement.

3. Work-Related Skills

While accomplishments focus on quantifiable results you have already achieved, work-related skills demonstrate what you can do in the future. This is an important category for potential employers because it is your skill set that shows whether or not you have the tools and aptitude to succeed once on the job. Interviewers may love your personality, and be impressed by your accomplishments, but if they don't think you have the right tools to succeed, they won't employ you. With this in mind, it is absolutely critical that you take the time to summarise the work-related skills you possess. When articulating your skills, there are two areas you should consider: your cognitive (thinking) skills and your functional skills (what you can do).

1   Cognitive skills describe the capabilities of your mind and personality and provide insight into your thought processes. Examples of cognitive skills include problem-solving skills, interpersonal skills and creative skills.

2   Functional skills describe what you are physically capable of doing on the job. Examples of functional skills include managing people, reducing expenses, implementing computer rollouts, developing budgets, quality control, report generation, large account sales, graphic design and customer service.

Those of you who don't have work experience should focus more on your cognitive skills than functional skills. If you have experience, then employers will probably focus more heavily on your functional abilities. Regardless of what position you interview for, interviewers will expect to see some sort of evidence that you have the skills and aptitude necessary to perform effectively on the job.

Demonstrate quantifiable evidence of your skills

If you think you possess a particular skill, prepare some examples of results from your previous experience to prove your case. Interviewers are going to expect you to provide proof of your claims, so it's best to be prepared. Let's say you believe that you have phenomenal selling skills. Evidence such as 'grew sales by double-digits during the last fiscal year' or 'achieved quota three years in a row' would be appropriate. If you have a unique ability to reduce expenses, include the amount by which you reduced expenses in your previous job, such as 'went out for bid and saved the corporation £10,000' or 'implemented a new phone system allowing the company to reduce staff by 10% and save more than £75,000 per year'. If you have fantastic management skills, then give examples such as 'reduced employee turnover by 25%' and 'increased productivity by 14%'.

Insider Tip
When managers create a position, they compile a list of criteria that they would like to see in an ideal candidate. Work-related skills typically are the foundation for this list.

4. Job-Related Knowledge And Credentials

Job-related knowledge is learned in school and on the job, and will help you succeed in the position you are trying to get. Unlike the other categories of strengths and competencies, career knowledge focuses more on what you know rather than on what you have done or can do. Those of you without strong work experience should put more emphasis on career knowledge in your interviews. If you are trying to get a job in the computer industry, knowledge, such as knowing a specific programming language, or a credential, such as a certification in a certain operating system, may be beneficial. If you were applying for an inventory management position, knowledge such as 'Just-In-Time' (JIT) and 'Vertical Process Management' would be more appropriate. If you want to go into marketing, you had better know the Four Ps of the Marketing Mix. Simply look back throughout your career and summarise your key elements of knowledge that will be most applicable for the job you are trying to get. Perhaps you know how to use spreadsheets and word processing software. If you are interviewing for an accounting position this knowledge could be very beneficial. However, if you were interviewing for a firefighter or security position, this would not be as applicable.

What makes you great?

Don't wait until an interview to list what makes you great. Start now by brainstorming about all your strengths and competencies, using the four cornerstones we have discussed. Remember: the more you focus on the good in you and your life, the better the outcomes will be. Write down as many core strengths and competencies as possible. Below, I have created a few simple worksheets for you to use. Try to keep your descriptions to four words or less. In doing this, you will gain focus, build your confidence and be more realistic in identifying the kinds of jobs you can get. After this exercise, you will realise that you truly are a spectacular person, and you'll be more motivated throughout your job hunt.

Insider Tip
Throughout your job hunt, interviewers will ask 'Why should I employ you?' By using the four cornerstones of defining your personal strengths and competencies, you'll be able to tell them why.

Strengths and Competencies

Worksheet 1

General Personality Traits:
(outgoing, social, empathetic, creative, motivated, etc.)

1

2

3

Work-Related Personality Traits:
(team-oriented, conscientious, detail-oriented, multi-tasking, etc.)

1

2

3

Personal Accomplishments:
(charity, fraternity, community service, etc.)

1

2

3

Job-Related Accomplishments:
(manager's award, featured in a company newsletter, etc.)

1

2

3

Worksheet 2

Cognitive Skills:
(interpersonal, problem-solving, creativity, etc.)

1

2

3

Functional Skills:
(managing people, reducing expenses, processing payroll, large-account sales, etc.)

1

2

3

Job-Related Knowledge:
(collections, year-end reporting, procurement, marketing, accounting, advertising, etc.)

1

2

3

Job-Related Credentials:
(certifications, degrees, diplomas, etc.)

1

2

3

Worksheet 2 *(continued)*

Other marketable skills and competencies:

1

2

3

4

5

6

7

8

9

10

Convert your strengths and competencies into benefits

Congratulations! By identifying your strengths and competencies, you have taken a major step towards a successful job search. However, identifying your positive attributes is only half the battle. You also need to be able to articulate how your strengths and competencies will benefit your potential employers.

Think about some of the jobs for which you might want to interview. Put yourself in the shoes of an interviewer. If you were the interviewer, what kind of strengths and competencies would you want your ideal candidates to possess? Why? Then, think about how these skills and aptitudes would benefit the company in relation to the other candidates having those skills and aptitudes. What would you come up with? On your interviews, not only are you going to have to relate your strengths and competencies, you are going to have to convert them into selling points that will make companies want to employ you!

> **Insider Tip**
> Your key selling points and their related benefits are what
> interviewers are looking for when they ask 'Why should
> I employ you over other candidates I am considering?'

If you are about to graduate from university or college

A success might be how you led a group to achieving a high mark
for a project. Your selling points might be your leadership skills and
your ability to work as a team player. The benefit may be that you'll
be easily integrated into the company and will work well with others.
Maybe you developed a website for a year group or organisation.
Selling points here could be your knowledge of Web design and your
ability to manage projects; a benefit may be your ability to make an
immediate contribution. Were you in charge of fundraising for your
school or alumni organisation? If so, you exhibited leadership when
coordinating people for a common effort. You exhibited creativity
when forming the idea that raised funds. It took teamwork to achieve
a goal. You were successful in that you raised more money than ever
before. You were marketing savvy when drawing so many people;
and demonstrated your sales skills to get those people to participate
and donate. A benefit may be your ability to generate new sales and
marketing programmes.

Work experience

If you have work experience, recall accomplishments from your
current and previous jobs. How about the time you turned that
irate customer into a happy customer, saving a huge order? Maybe
you were given an excellent appraisal. How about the note you
received from a colleague who was grateful for your help on a
project? Or maybe you excelled and won a corporate award.

Come up with a minimum of four strengths and competencies and
generate at least one key selling point for each one. From that selling
point, quantify what the benefit will be to the company looking to
employ you. For example, let's say you are a plant supervisor.

Perhaps one of your strengths is that you are a great cost cutter. First come up with a quantifiable example: 'I cut the cost of manufacturing by 25% on XYZ product for ABC Company.' Now summarise the selling point in terms that would be applicable to the job for which you are interviewing.

Finally, articulate the benefits that the company will receive (the 'so what'). Why should the company care about this selling point? Here is an example: 'If I saved you just 10% of your cost of manufacturing, the savings alone would more than pay my salary.'

Everyone has strengths and competencies that can land a job!

Good interviewers will ask you about your strengths and why they are applicable to the opportunity at hand. So, think about the job you really want. Now, go back to your personal strength worksheet and decide what are your three most relevant strengths and competencies to that position. Write them down and quantify them. Come up with some tangible examples that illustrate your selling points. Finally, summarise how those selling points will benefit your potential employers.

Key selling points worksheet

Strength No. 1:

Key selling point:

Benefits to company:

Strength No. 2:

Key selling point:

Benefits to company:

Strength No. 3:

Key selling point:

Benefits to company:

Checklist Summary

✓ Focus on building a solid foundation.
✓ Be aware of your feelings and the energy created.
✓ Identify your strengths and competencies using the four cornerstones.
✓ Complete the strengths and competencies worksheet.
✓ Quantify your most relevant attributes.
✓ Convert those attributes into benefits.
✓ Complete the Key Selling Points Worksheet.

'When you start each day with gratitude, you tune into a positive frequency that'll attract success and happiness into your life and your job hunt.'

Secret No. 3
Define the Job You Really Want

- Identify your likes and dislikes
- Explore your four Ps of career alignment
- Define your ideal job using the 10 elements of job satisfaction.

Now that you know your strengths and competencies, you should have a good idea of the jobs you can get. But what type of career do you really want?

Defining the job you want is one of the most important secrets to a successful job search. After all, if you don't know what you want, how are you going to get it?

Recently, I volunteered to critique CVs at a job fair. Out of almost 100 people, I would say at least 40 had absolutely no idea what they wanted to do for a living and couldn't articulate why someone should employ them. In looking at their CVs, I had to ask questions such as 'What kind of job do you want?' and 'What message are you trying to convey?' In just 15 seconds, I could ascertain that many of these people had no focus or direction. My response was 'If you don't know what you want or what you are good at, how is an interviewer supposed to know?' You can't expect other people to be able to work this out for you.

> 'You have to come to your own conclusions. It is up to you to tell them.'

Your Ideal Job

Sadly, most people believe there is no such thing as an ideal job. They never take the time to define their ultimate position, and then they wonder why they cannot ever find a job they can enjoy. In fact, the reason so many people have difficulty finding overall happiness in life is that they never take the time to define what they need and want in life in order to be happy. If you don't make the time to define the traits and attributes of your ideal job, boss and life, you are destined to a life of mediocrity.

Causes Of Job Dissatisfaction

Most people dislike their current jobs because they accepted positions just to earn some money, rather than those in alignment with their personal interests, skills, passions, values. They can do these jobs but lack the motivation and desire to do their jobs well, and, as a result, they end up unhappy and are often sacked. Have you ever taken the time to define your ideal job? If not, you should! Investing the time to define your ideal job will be one of the wisest investments you will ever make.

Live to work or work to live

Including commuting time (on average, up to one hour each way) and actual work (usually eight hours a day), most people spend approximately 50 hours a week working. Because the average person sleeps around 56 hours a week, they consume 106 hours a week working and sleeping. There are only 168 hours in a week. That leaves only 62 hours a week of 'free' time. Hmm . . . 50 hours on work . . . 62 hours for pleasure. You spend almost half your waking hours working and commuting! If you don't enjoy your occupation, the stress, frustration and lack of fulfilment is going to negatively impact on the other facets of your life outside the job. It is critical to have a job that you can enjoy rather than a job that just pays the bills.

The most important aspects of my life are health, love, family, friends and spirituality – and then my job. But if my job is not enjoyable, that negatively impacts on everything else. Feelings such as jealousy, embarrassment, lethargy and frustration take over my thoughts when I am not doing something I enjoy. Consequently, throughout my career I've always tried to choose professions where I could look forward to work as much as I do leisure. It's very important to me that I have a job I can be proud of. Rightly or wrongly, we often derive our well-being and self-worth from our occupations. These evaluations do not have to be related to money. The ultimate satisfaction is doing work that you enjoy and that is in alignment with your goals, beliefs and desired lifestyle.

Work Can Be Fun!

You can actually enjoy work! As simple as it sounds, the key to enjoying your occupation is to be in the right job for you. When you are in the right job doing something you are passionate about, it no longer feels like work. One of the reasons I have always loved selling-related professions is that for me it is like playing a game every day. Before I founded my own company, I had several jobs that I was truly passionate about and loved. I remember times, in those jobs, when I couldn't wait for Monday. Have you ever been able to say that?

The best job I had, before starting my business, was when I was a director of a £70 million division for American Power Conversion (APC). In this role I managed their OEM (Original Equipment Manufacturer) effort, focusing on accounts such as IBM, Dell, Hewlett-Packard and Gateway.

We were in an extremely competitive marketplace and I was fortunate to have a team of sales 'all-stars' working for me. It was as if we were playing in a championship game every day. The position was challenging and rewarding. It allowed me to travel the globe at the company's expense. And thanks to the quality of my team and the strategies we employed, we consistently had the highest revenue growth and market-share increases in the company.

For years, the job was a dream. Not only was I doing something I loved, I had an excellent income. Then it all changed. The company went through a major reorganisation of its management. Unfortunately, the new managers took a lot of the fun and independence out of the position. They started to dictate how I should manage my people and run my business according to political reasons, rather than sound business rationale.

I had always said to myself that once I left APC, I would have to start my own business. I just couldn't envision another situation where I could have been as passionate. But not everyone wants the pressure or hassles that come as a result of being their own boss. I'd be lying to you if I said there weren't times when I questioned my own decision to quit and start my own business.

Most people want to find a job they can enjoy while working for a successful company. It is very possible to find an ideal job working for someone else, as long as you know what it is that you want. You, too, can find the same passion I had working for APC. Visualise having a job you can enjoy. What would that job be? What kind of qualities and characteristics would that job have? What kind of a boss would you be working for? Would you be working for a small or big company? Would you be working out of the office or in the home? The following is a list of some job characteristics I value. After reviewing my list, try creating one of your own.

Characteristics I value

- Freedom to work as if I were my own boss
- Challenging, not boring
- Involves domestic and international travel
- Competitive
- Company is a leader in its industry
- Colleagues are talented, driven and motivated
- Financially rewarding
- Provides recognition and appreciation
- Matches my values and beliefs.

What Characteristics Are Important To You?

Once you find a position that closely matches your desires and beliefs, you will actually look forward to going to work each day. This enjoyment will positively impact on everything else in your life. Throughout my career, I have found three exercises to be extremely beneficial in identifying the ideal job:

1 Identify likes and dislikes
2 Explore the four Ps of career alignment
3 Define the ideal job using the 10 elements of job satisfaction.

Exercise 1: Identify your likes and dislikes

One of the best ways to work out what you really want to do for a living is to take a step back, reflect on your previous positions and bosses, and identify what you liked and what you didn't like. Once you capture those thoughts, you can try to find new opportunities that will maximise your likes while minimising your dislikes. What positions and bosses did you like? Which ones didn't you like? If you are just graduating from university and you haven't had any jobs in the past, then reflect on your previous courses and instructors.

I first tried this exercise when I decided to leave IBM. Even though I had loved working for IBM, and I was a top performer, I became disenchanted because of the remuneration. Every year IBM kept doubling my sales quota, without wanting to pay me more money. I had no problem with an increased quota. But I was not happy with getting less money to sell more.

When I decided that I wanted to leave, I put together a spreadsheet to try to define my ideal job. I listed all the things I enjoyed about the job that I currently had . . . and all the things I wanted in a future job. Then I ranked each in order of importance.

Some of my desires for a new job

- A top-drawer boss like the one I had at IBM
- A job that involves travel
- A job with a market-leader and high-quality firm like IBM
- A job where, if successful, I could earn a good income
- A position that was truly pay-for-performance.

I also wanted to have share options in the company for which I work. When I put together this list, it was at the beginning of the bull market of the 1990s and share options were just becoming popular. I desired a job where I could utilise the experience and contacts I had developed over the years at IBM.

As a result of doing the exercise, I was extremely focused. I knew exactly the type of position I wanted. In fact, within two weeks of deciding to leave IBM, I had received three job offers, all in the same week. I ended up choosing American Power Conversion (APC), where I enjoyed seven fantastic and rewarding years.

Your favourite jobs or courses

What were the traits of your favourite jobs or courses? Who were your favourite bosses or teachers and why? Capture these thoughts. Write them down or create a spreadsheet. Later in this chapter, I will provide you with a worksheet (see page 44) to summarise these reflections.

Your least favourite jobs or courses

What did you dislike about your least favourite job or course? Why was it so demotivating? You will find that once you put some of these things down on paper, you can get a better understanding of what you enjoy, and what you don't.

Sometimes it's harder to work out what we really want than it is to decide what we don't want. Ideally, you want to find a job that maximises the things you desire and minimises the aspects you'd like to avoid. It sounds simple, but you'd be surprised at how many people end up in the same dead-end positions because they don't take the time to articulate their likes and dislikes.

I worked at APC more than twice as long as any other company because the job had all the traits I loved, and very few of those that I hated. In fact, when I first took the job at APC, it had every one of the traits I outlined as 'wants' on my spreadsheet. It wasn't until almost seven years later that the negatives began to outweigh the positives. But, let's face it, in this day and age, lasting seven years at one company isn't bad.

Summarise Your Thoughts

The following is a worksheet you can use to capture your reflections. The purpose of this exercise is very simple: identify what you like and what you don't like. I know this isn't 'rocket science', but when you look for a new job, ideally you really want to find one that has more of the things you like and less of the things you don't like.

Identify Your Likes And Dislikes

Worksheet 1

What were your most favourite jobs or courses?

What traits made these the most favourite? (freedom, rewarding, travel, pay, challenge, team, etc.)

Who were your favourite bosses or teachers?

What attributes did you like most about these bosses or teachers? (appreciative, mentoring, open-minded, friendly, etc.)

Identify Your Likes And Dislikes

Worksheet 2

What were your least favourite jobs or courses?

What traits made these your least favourite?
(politics, bureaucracy, remuneration, effort required, time required, etc.)

Who were your least favourite bosses or teachers?

What attributes did you like least about these bosses or teachers?
(narrow-minded, political, over-aggressive, lack of compassion, etc.)

Your Four Ps

Right now, the universe has given you a gift. You have the opportunity to find the job of your dreams, one that you can be truly passionate about and one that allows you to be all that you can be.

Exercise 2: The Four Ps of career alignment

The second exercise I have found to be helpful in defining an
ideal job is to explore what I call the Four Ps of career alignment:
purpose, passions, principles and possibilities. Purpose is why you
are here. Passions are what really motivate you. Principles are the
values that are important to you. Possibilities are all the jobs in
life that you are capable of doing with the talent you possess.

- Purpose
- Principles
- Passions
- Possibilities.

Have you lost your job? Are you unhappy in your current
position? If so, probably (if you are honest with yourself) it is
because the job is/was not in alignment with one of your Four
Ps. After all, if you aren't passionate about what you are doing,
it's hard to get excited about going to work. It's equally difficult
if you are employed on a job that goes against your morals or
values. Also, if you are doing something that doesn't properly
utilise the talent you have, the odds are that you won't be happy.

Think about the Four Ps and write down a couple of examples,
that are important to you, for each one.

Purpose

I am a firm believer that we were all put on this earth for a reason. It
would be nice if we were told exactly why we are here on our birth
certificate. Unfortunately life doesn't work that way. If you have never
asked yourself what your life's purpose is, now is a great opportunity
to do so. Not working in alignment with your purpose can cause
great discomfort and dissatisfaction. When I first went into my own
business, I went into day trading. I had always been intrigued by the
stock market and I thought, what an easy way to make a ton of money!
Wow, was I wrong. Interestingly enough, I kept sabotaging myself.

Every time I was making money too easily, I would make a deal I knew I shouldn't make. For some reason, I would do it anyway and I would end up giving back most of my profits.

I was a good trader and I could read a stock chart with the best of them. But for some reason, I kept sabotaging my efforts. Finally, I decided to take a break from trading and go on a trip, by myself, to do some serious soul-searching.

I wanted to get to the bottom of why day trading wasn't working out even though I had the talent to succeed. During that trip, I took out a blank notebook and started reflecting on my four Ps. I really wanted to get to the bottom of my self-sabotaging efforts. What is my life's purpose?

The answer I kept coming up with was that I was put on this earth to help people who want to be successful. This was interesting because, in my mind, day trading wasn't helping anyone but me. Yes, I would try to justify to myself that I was helping others by providing liquidity to the market, but the bottom line was I didn't believe it.

Principles

What are my core principles or values? I came up with values such as giving, loving, competitiveness, trustworthiness, honesty, passion and sharing. This was a major revelation. The only way to be giving, loving and sharing in day trading is to lose money. Wow, no wonder I kept sabotaging my efforts! Every time I was trying to deceive the market on a deal or I was making money, I was going against my core values. When I made money, I wasn't giving; I was taking. When I tried to fake out a market maker, I wasn't being honest; I was being dishonest.

Day trading was clearly out of alignment with my life's purpose as well as my core principles. Knowing that, I could no longer trade for a living. This left me in a state of shock and I had to ask myself, okay, now what am I going to do? At first, I was stumped. Then I thought, why don't I write down all the things I enjoy doing and see if I can come up with some conclusions?

Passions

I wrote down a list of things I enjoyed doing in my previous jobs. I then composed a list of aspects I enjoyed doing that weren't necessarily just job-related, such as travel and being around friends. In other words, I compiled a list of my passions.

My list included things such as teaching, mentoring, travelling, selling, working with others, competing, being creative and making my own decisions. This was very revealing as day trading allowed me few of these passions. Yes, it was competitive and allowed me to make my own decisions, but there was no teaching, mentoring, working with others, or travelling. It was Todd against the world, and I didn't like that.

So I came up with a great list of wants. Now what?

Possibilities

What are my possibilities? What jobs could I do, with the talent I have, that would be in alignment with my other three Ps of purpose, principles and passions?

I came up with a list of options such as becoming a teacher, going back into sales, becoming a professional speaker, going into property sales, and even considered going back to work for my old company. I had many opportunities from which to choose. Ultimately, I chose what I am doing today.

The Four Ps worksheet

What is your life's purpose?
(help others, teach, bring up a family, motivate others, solve a world problem, etc.)

What are your core principles (values)?
(family, success, honesty, trustworthiness, etc.)

What are your passions?
(freedom, creativity, competition, travel, entertaining, etc.)

What are your possibilities?
(doctor, teacher, salesperson, accountant, firefighter, graphic
designer, etc.)

Limit Your Focus

I am sure there are scores of jobs you are capable of doing, but what
do you really want to do? Earlier I took you through a reflection
exercise, looking into the likes and dislikes of previous positions and
asked you to explore your four Ps of career alignment. Now is the time
to narrow your focus down to one or two jobs that you really want to
do for a living.

Focus on one or two types of jobs

I suggest trying to focus on only one or two types of occupations (not one
or two companies) that you want to work at, such as customer service and
sales, or technical support and network management. It is difficult enough
to be passionate about just one position at a time, let alone multiple ones.
Expanding your scope beyond two is nearly impossible.

You will be competing against candidates who know exactly what
they want to do for a living. They are going to be very good at

articulating why they should be hired. If your concentration is too diluted, you won't have a chance when in competition with those who are more focused. Interviewers aren't stupid; they can tell right away who is passionate about an opportunity and who is interviewing just to find a job that'll pay the bills. Interviewers want someone with passion who will put everything they have into the job and hopefully stay with a company for years. Most managers hate turnover and lethargy.

Exercise 3: Define Your Ideal Job

One of the best ways to limit the focus of your job hunt is to use a methodology that considers the 10 elements of job satisfaction. I have used this process throughout my career to determine what I really wanted to do for a living. Once you go through this process and consider these key elements, you will be much more focused throughout your job search.

1 Occupation.
2 Industry.
3 Company.
4 Career path.
5 Structure.
6 Hours.
7 Travel.
8 Environment.
9 Location.
10 Remuneration and benefits.

---

1. Occupation

The first element is to define the exact type of job that really interests you. The best way to do this is to look at your list of possibilities. From this list determine which occupations allow you to best utilise your strengths. Which of these jobs can you see yourself going to each day? What jobs really interest you? Job satisfaction is in the eye of the beholder.

For example, if your passion in life is cleaning and organising, being a housekeeper may appeal to you. Driving a lorry could be tempting to someone who likes to travel, see the country and meet new people. Software development can be ideal for someone who loves the challenge of taking a new concept and turning it into a successful product.

Only you know where your passion resides. Don't listen to what others say and think you should be. Had I listened to others, I would have gone to medical school to become a doctor. But I get woozy at the sight of blood and medical instruments. I don't think I would have lasted too long in medical school! Medicine is not my passion.

Decide what interests you. There are millions of ways to earn a living. People who like their jobs tend to live longer and happier lives than those who detest going to work each day. Job stress causes people to lose sleep and lead unhealthy lifestyles. When I am under pressure or frustrated, often that unhappiness manifests itself as illness. My worst maladies have always coincided with times I was most stressed about my job.

Typically, people who constantly complain about their jobs don't feel in control of their own destiny. Often, they will stay in jobs they dislike their entire lives because they feel that every job will lead to dissatisfaction. Don't let that become your reality.

It is possible to enjoy going to work each day when you choose an occupation that is in alignment with your passions and pleasures. I enjoy work time almost more than my leisure time because I love helping and interacting with other people, and I thrive on competition and the thrill of the ride. I have worked in situations I hated, and that's why I left those jobs.

Life is too short to do something you don't enjoy. So, clear your mind and think about the following questions.

■ What jobs allow you to best capitalise on your core strengths and unique selling points?
■ If you could do any occupation in the world, what would you choose?

2. Industry

Once you have decided on the type of job that interests you, your next goal is to determine your ideal industry. When I graduated from university, I received six job offers. I knew I wanted to be a salesperson, but what did I want to sell?

The two offers that interested me most were from NCR (a computer manufacturer) and U.S. Steel (a leader in the steel industry). U.S. Steel offered me a starting salary of 25% more than NCR. Essentially, the choice boiled down to whether I wanted to be in the steel industry or the computer industry.

I chose the computer industry and accepted the offer from NCR, even though it offered less money. I have never regretted that decision. Both were tremendous companies. I just opted for the industry that interested me the most at the time. Before starting my business, I spent 14 years in the computer industry – and loved it! I thrived on the constant change, abundant opportunities and rapid innovations.

Just one decision can change your entire life. Choosing an industry is not a decision to be made lightly. Had I chosen the steel industry, my whole life would have been different – not just my career, but also my experiences, my friends, and even where I would have lived. Perhaps more importantly, once you choose an industry, depending on the industry and career, you will probably remain in that industry for a minimum of three job cycles. Because of the experience and knowledge that is gained through each job, rarely do people switch industries. Once expertise is acquired, it is very difficult to discard that investment, switch industries and risk being unable to apply that knowledge to a new area. Does this sound scary? It's true. So take some time and know what really interests you. Ask yourself, with my strengths, experiences and key selling points, which industries should I consider?

There are thousands of different industries you can choose from. Let's say you wanted to go into customer service. Well, banks have customer service departments, so do manufacturers, doctors, insurers, hotels and scores of other industries.

Some major industry classifications

- Manufacturing
- Information Technology
- Accounting
- Law
- Retail
- Finance
- Hospitality
- Healthcare.

As you might guess, often there is quite a bit of overlap between one industry and another. For instance, computer specialists are needed in any industry. Lawyers are needed regardless of the type of business.

The main point is to identify what industries interest you. If you want to be a lawyer, do you want corporate law or property law? If you want to go into marketing, do you want to work for an agency or a manufacturer? Do you want to focus on consumer goods or industrial? There are typically scores of industries you can choose from in almost any occupation.

3. Company

Next, ask yourself what type of company you want to join. Do you seek a company that promotes from within or one that hires from the outside? What kind of management philosophies do you value? Do you want the prestige of a big established company or do you want the challenge and opportunity that a smaller start-up offers?

Prestige and opportunity for training and growth come with working for a company with a household name. However, big companies also have a lot of politics, bureaucracies and rules. What is more important to you? These are important issues to consider when deciding the type of company that is right for you. There are always trade-offs.

The key is to define a type of company that has more of what you want and less of what you don't want. It sounds so simple. But I cannot tell you how many people hop from job to job and always end up working for the same type of company. If you hate politics and bureaucracies, yet you keep getting jobs in large companies, what is the likelihood you will ever be happy? Size and type of company both play major roles in job satisfaction. What kind of company do you want to work for?

4. Career Path

Now that you have decided your ideal job, industry and type of company, your next decision is to determine which career path to take. This will be your road map (plan). Choose a career path leading to a good future. No one wants a dead-end job.

While nothing that relates to careers is ever written in stone, it is important to decide early on in your job-hunting process what kind of path you want to take. What is your ultimate destination? Some people want to be an engineer their entire career. Others want to become a manager. Some want to shoot for the top and become the leader of a company. What do you want? Be honest with yourself. Society puts pressure on us to go into management, but these positions can come with a lot of headaches. There is something to be said for leaving the job at the office at the end of the day.

If you think you want to go into management, do you have the strengths and expertise to do so now? If not, are you capable of learning what you need to know to succeed? If the answer is yes, interview with companies that are growing and promote from within. Then, identify the types of jobs that will give you the experience you'll need to become a manager in that company.

If you want to be in sales your entire career, research industries and companies with the highest salaries, the best perks and the most promising futures for their top salespeople. For instance, in the 1980s everyone wanted to get into property. In the 1990s in the United States, Enterprise software and Year 2000 software sales positions were most in demand. But what happened to Year 2000 software salespeople after the year 2000?

Who knows . . .

Insider Tip
In almost 85% of all job interviews, you will be asked,
'Where do you want to be in five years?' If you are not,
you'll undoubtedly be asked a similar one. By determining
your ideal career path now, you will be prepared when this
question comes up in your interviews.

5. Structure

Although you know the type of job that you want, similar jobs can
have totally different structures. For example, in sales you can have a
job that is a part of a team or one where you are on your own. You can
have remuneration based on 'management by objectives' (MBO) or
remuneration based strictly on sales revenue or sales growth.

What kind of job structure is ideal for you? Do you want a job
with set goals and objectives? Do you want a job where you are
told exactly what to do? Or do you want one where you help in
determining ongoing strategic decisions? Maybe you want a job where
you are part of a team and are compensated according to the team's
successes. Conversely, you might prefer a situation where you work
independently and are recognised solely for your own efforts. Do you
want to work on short-term or long-term projects?

You've heard the expression 'you can't place a square peg in a
round hole'. If you take a job that doesn't match the structure you are
looking for, you will feel like a square peg. Typically, 'square pegs'
become disgruntled and end up always complaining about their jobs.
You don't want that, do you? This is why it is so important to identify
the kind of structure that is best suited for you.

6. Hours

Have you ever thought about how long and how hard you want to
work? Do you mind working 50 to 60 hours per week? Or would
you rather work only 40 hours? Do you want to work part time or
full time?

Many jobs today require far more than the traditional 9–5 schedule. Often you can be required to work long hours, late at night, and sometimes on weekends. Is that a sacrifice you are willing to make?

Examples of professions that require extensive hours are accounting, consulting, legal, healthcare, retail, property sales and hotel management. It is up to you. If you value balance in your life or if you have children, then work hours may be important to you. If you are one who wants to succeed and climb the career ladder at all costs, then work hours may not be a big deal. Either way, you need to decide how much you really want to work.

7. Travel

Another factor to consider when looking for a job is travel. Some jobs require extensive travel. Others demand little or no travel. If you enjoy travelling, then a desk job may not appeal to you. However, if you have a family you don't want to be away from, it may be best to have a job where you go to the same location every day.

As it turned out, one of the things I didn't like about day trading was that I had to go to the same place every day to trade. Some people like that concept. I'd rather be in a situation where I can have multiple working environments. What would you prefer?

8. Environment

Many people enjoy working because of the mental stimulation they get from being around other motivated people. If you like being around others, then a large office environment may be optimal. Some like the freedom of working on their own without the need for direct supervision. In this case, working out of the home may be more appealing.

Do you want to work at a corporate headquarters, a regional hub, or a remote office? A remote location is ideal if you want to remain independent. However, if you want to get promoted and be on the fast track, you may want to be at headquarters where you are visible to key corporate managers and your contributions can be seen first hand.

Do you want to work in an office building or out of your home? An office provides camaraderie and close proximity to your boss. However, working out of the home offers more autonomy. Perhaps best of all, because you don't have to commute, working out of the home allows you to have more time to yourself. But that comes at a cost. You lose the opportunity to meet as many new people as you would in an office environment.

What aspects are most important to you? Are you comfortable in a cubicle or do you need your own office? Some people enjoy working with background noise; others need the silence of an office. Often, people in jobs such as telemarketing, accounting, customer service, procurement, engineering and administration are placed in cubicles. Others, such as lawyers, doctors, managers, and those in human resources/personnel, have their own offices.

Do you want to wear business casual or business formal attire? While I enjoy wearing casual clothing, other people enjoy dressing more formally. Which style is more comfortable for you? Clothing often can have a major influence on productivity. Some air stewards and stewardesses can be so chipper wearing their cheerful, smart uniforms.

The bottom line is your work environment, be it your office or your clothes, all of which has a major impact on job satisfaction and performance.

9. Location

In today's global economy, you can end up receiving job offers from all over the world. Have you ever thought about where you want to live? Often people move to another city strictly for a job. Before you do that, you need to be honest with yourself about what is important in your life.

I used to think my career was the most important aspect of my life, that it didn't matter where I lived or worked, until I relocated to Raleigh, North Carolina, for a job promotion. Before my move, Raleigh was named the top region (to live) in the country. Thousands of people were flocking there. I took the promotion without having ever seen Raleigh. I was filled with excitement.

At the time of my move, I was single. I didn't know one person who lived in Raleigh, but that didn't matter to me. All I could see were the big dollar signs of a great promotion. The first year, the job went fantastically well. I was earning more than ever before, had success and recognition within the company and travelled to exciting places. But during the beginning of my second year in Raleigh, I started to question my decision. Even though I was earning a good income, I was not happy. I started to feel a void in my life.

At first, I had no idea why I was feeling so empty inside. After much introspection, I finally realised that I really missed my family and friends. I didn't recognise how important a local support structure was to me – until I no longer had it.

Until then, I didn't understand the importance of balance in my life. Finally, I understood that work and money were not the sole sources of happiness. I realised that health, love, family, friends and spirituality were far more important to me than the job. Unfortunately, it took getting relocated to Raleigh for me to discover this.

Thankfully, I moved back to Chicago. Within a couple of months of my return, my mother became very sick. Ultimately, less than two years later, she passed away. Had I stayed in Raleigh, I would have missed out on the time I was able to spend with my dear mother during those final two years of her life.

If you are close to your family, you may want to live and work in the same area as they do. If not, at least the internet and phone provide ways to stay in touch. Only you know where you want to live and how important it is for you to be near your family and friends. Every place has positives and negatives. I recommend that before you pick up and move for a job, ask yourself if you can still keep balance in your life. Then ask yourself if you can still live within the values of what is important to you. I'll bet you didn't realise how many dynamics you should consider when thinking about your ideal job.

10. Remuneration And Benefits

The 10th and final element to consider is the one that pays your bills and puts a roof over your head: remuneration and benefits. You might love your job, but if you are not making enough money to live the lifestyle you want, you won't be happy. When looking at remuneration and benefits, there are several areas you should consider.

Wages

Wages are the first thing to consider when choosing an opportunity. After all, our wages pay the bills. Often, the lifestyle we live dictates how much we need to earn. How much do you want to make? How much do you realistically need to earn to live your ideal lifestyle? Do you want a salary or a pay-by-the-hour position? Some positions offer the chance to earn overtime. Is overtime important to you?

Remuneration structure

There are many ways a company can compensate employees. Some firms pay employees hourly, while others pay a salary. Do you want an hourly job or one based on salary? Depending on the occupation, the remuneration structure can include some form of leverage. This leverage can come in the form of a bonus or commission.

The idea with leverage is that the better you perform on the job, the more money you make. Typically in leveraged positions, companies pay you a lesser salary but the total you can earn can be more if you hit certain goals and objectives. Are you willing to risk a portion of your salary for the leverage to earn more if you succeed?

If you choose a profession that has leveraged remuneration, do you want weekly, monthly, quarterly or annual bonuses? Or do you want a commission-based job? If so, do you want a salary plus commission? Or are you willing to take a straight commission job where you can earn more money if you perform well?

The key is to decide what structure works best for you. If you expect to work long hours, taking an hourly job that pays overtime might be better for you than a salary job that doesn't pay overtime. If you expect to excel on the job, then perhaps taking a position in which a portion of the remuneration is leveraged would be better for you than one without any risk. Either way, it is important to determine what structure works best for you.

Profit sharing

Profit sharing is when a company literally shares a percentage of its earnings with the employees. Many companies pay slightly lower salaries to their employees, but then allow them to receive sometimes significant bonuses based on the profit of the organisation.

When the company is profitable, employees can make a higher overall wage than comparable employees in other organisations. Are you willing to risk a portion of your salary to earn potentially more money with profit sharing?

Allowances

Depending on the job and company, a position can come with an allowance or multiple ones. Allowances are a means, outside of salary and bonus, to compensate employees for expenses incurred while on the job. The most common allowances paid are for working out of the home (home office) and for extensive driving (car) and relocation expenses.

Do you want to work out of your home? If so, do you have room in your house to work? How much of a housing allowance would you need to make it worthwhile? What if the company will let you work from home, but they make you responsible for all expenses? Would you still take the job? Are you prepared to deal with the complicated tax implications of allowances for working from home?

Does the occupation require you to drive frequently? If so, will you be compensated for the wear and tear on your car? Would you want a monthly car allowance or to receive payments by the mileage you drive? If you get a car allowance, are you willing to let the company dictate the kind of car you drive? Maybe you want nothing short of being provided with a company car. But if that's the case, your choice of models will be quite limited.

If your job involves relocation to another part of the country or abroad, does the company offer to cover all relocation expenses? Or do they offer only to cover actual removal expenses? But suppose you don't want to move, you want to let your own house and live in rented accommodation – will they cover that too, as an option?

In any event, allowances can contribute significantly to your bottom line. One of the reasons I chose to work for APC was that I received a $400 (£275 approx) housing allowance and a $300 (£200 approx) car allowance. That made a huge impact, because I still needed to pay for my car and housing anyway. To me, that was like found money and definitely had an impact on my decision.

Share options

Share options give employees the right to purchase company shares at a specified price, over a particular period of time. Some companies use options as a way of rewarding top performers, reducing employee turnover and increasing employee productivity. When a company's shares go down, the options are worthless.

Many companies place restrictions on when you can exercise your options. I had a friend who worked for a wireless communications company. After he joined the company, its shares skyrocketed and his options were worth more than $1 million on paper.

However, the company made him hold the options for an extended length of time before he could exercise them. Unfortunately, the shares crashed before he could exercise his options and his $1 million (£685,000 approx) evaporated before he could cash in on even a single dollar.

Companies can offer share options in lieu of higher salaries. Are you willing to sacrifice some salary for share options? Are the shares likely to increase? What is an optimal vesting period? How long do you have to hold the shares before you can sell? These are things to consider when comparing one job offer with another.

Retirement plans

Most companies offer some form of pension plan. But these can differ significantly from company to company. Some companies will offer a salary-related scheme, where your pension is based on your salary and the number of years you've paid into the scheme. Others may offer a money purchase scheme where your pension will be based on how much you've paid into the scheme and the returns on the investment of that money. What type of plan do you want? There are pros and cons to every plan.

As we saw in the late 1990s and early 2000s, many companies saw the funding for their retirement plans diminish. Thousands of employees saw their retirement savings vanish. When you are considering offers, you should look at the financial stability of each company and of their retirement plans. How is the plan funded? How secure is the plan? What is the likelihood that the plan will survive to pay the benefits you were promised?

Medical benefits

One area of the economy that has seen more inflation than almost anything else is private healthcare and private healthcare insurance. The costs of seeing a doctor privately have skyrocketed. Many companies, as a way to reduce expenses, have significantly cut back on their private healthcare benefits.

In my opinion, this is a big mistake. Nothing is more important than healthy employees. Employees are ultimately what makes or breaks the success of a business. Some firms have either asked employees to shoulder a percentage of the cost of the insurance or have reduced the quality of the programmes. Several have even eliminated these benefits altogether.

I have a couple of friends who have a child with a pre-existing condition that makes it very difficult to obtain medical insurance for the family. As a result, the quality of the healthcare programme is one of the most important aspects of remuneration and benefits that they consider.

What is your situation? How important is private medical insurance for you? It's important to decide early on in your job search what kind of healthcare insurance you need.

Pay rise policies

Every company has its own rules for how much of a pay rise employees can get come review time. Some companies have very strict policies that limit the amount of the increase employees can get, while others are more liberal. If you expect to be a top performer, a company's pay increase policy can be quite important.

Will you tolerate a company that limits its pay rises to 10% in exchange for more job security? Are you willing to work for a company where you have to 'walk on water' to get an increase, but you get great perks? What is your expectation of a fair pay rise policy?

I cannot overemphasise this point. If a company has a very strict policy, then you had better hold out for more money upfront. However, if the company is more liberal and believes in significantly rewarding performance, you may not have to get such a high offer. Once you sign on at a company, it is usually very difficult to significantly increase your earnings without getting a promotion, which makes the initial job offer and the pay rise policies important elements of the decision-making process.

Perks

Some companies offer employees small extras that can make a big difference in job satisfaction. These perks can range from corporate daycare, to expense accounts, golf club memberships and onsite exercise clubs, to discounts at local shops and education reimbursements. What are the important perks for you? Are you willing to sacrifice some perks for more pay? Or would you sacrifice some pay for more perks?

Remuneration Is The Number One Cause Of Employee Dissatisfaction

Before launching into your job search, you should develop a budget and work out what you need to earn in order to be happy with your job. While remuneration is not the sole determinant of job satisfaction, it carries significant weight. If you are making less than you feel you are worth, or less than required for the lifestyle you want, the odds are you won't be happy on the job.

Many people don't take the time to determine what they are worth and what they expect to earn. This is a big mistake. By quantifying your expectations before starting your job hunt, you will be much more focused and successful in finding a job that excites you.

Consider all aspects of remuneration, not just salary

Often, some companies make up for lower salary and bonus earnings by providing phenomenal benefits and perks. Some companies have their own daycare and exercise facilities. Others provide benefits such as country club memberships, increased maternity leave, more holiday time, and even free lunches on Fridays. These perks can save hundreds, if not thousands, of pounds every month.

Everything doesn't just boil down to salary. Once you know what you want, you will be much more focused, efficient and successful in your job hunt. Also, you will convey the image of a goal-oriented person. That will come across loud and clear in an interview, and will rank you above your competition.

Define Your Ideal Job Using The 10 Elements Of Job Satisfaction

While the 10 elements are fresh in your mind, list the characteristics you want in your ideal job. You can use the worksheet on page 65. Once you have identified your ideal job, try to summarise it in a one- to two-sentence personal mission statement.

If you read almost any corporate annual report, you will see a mission statement. This statement serves as the focus for the organisation. When you articulate a mission for your job hunt, it allows you to be more focused and direct in your job-hunting efforts.

Once you come up with a mission statement, post it on your wall and in your notebooks and journals. By focusing on your goal, and not the process, you will succeed. Finally, using the worksheets in this chapter, come up with a list of potential companies you can target in your job search.

'It is always easier to get to your destination when you know where you are going.'

Job Definition

Worksheet 1

Type of job(s):

1

2

3

Type of industry(s):

1

2

3

Type of company:

Private	☐	Public	☐
Established	☐	Entrepreneurial	☐
Conservative	☐	Liberal	☐
High growth	☐	Stable growth	☐
Large	☐	Small	☐

Desired career path:

Year 1.

Year 2.

Year 3.

Year 4.

Year 5.

Worksheet 2

Ideal job structure:

Desired work hours:
Per day
Per week

Travel: Yes/No
If yes, how much travel:

Work out of home or office?

Type of office environment desired:

Attire desired: casual or formal?

City(s)/locations you can work in:

Desired remuneration and benefits:

Ideal job mission statement:

Worksheet 3

Company brainstorm: (Unilever, Shell, GlaxoSmithKline, Tesco, Starbucks, etc.)

1

2

3

4

5

6

7

8

9

10

11

12

13

14

15

Checklist Summary

✓ Dissatisfaction is caused by a mismatch between values and job.
✓ Don't live to work. Work to live.
✓ Almost half your life is spent on work. Enjoy it.
✓ Only you can determine where your passion resides.
✓ Identify your likes and dislikes.
✓ Explore your Four Ps of career alignment.
✓ Before you search, define your ideal job using the 10 elements.
✓ Create a personal job-hunting mission statement.

'If you don't know what you want, how are you
going to get it?'

Secret No. 4

Justify Why You Should Be Recruited

- The 7-Step Recruitment Process
- Predict the decision-making criteria
- Create a business case to justify your employment.

Congratulations! You're doing fine! Thus far, you have already built a solid foundation for a successful job search. By believing in yourself, identifying your core strengths and competencies, and defining your ideal job, you are now well on your way towards getting the job you really want. That brings us to the next phase of the job-hunting process: justifying why you should be hired.

'Back in the good old days' it used to be that you could almost just show up for the interview and get the job. That certainly isn't the case anymore.

'Times are for ever changing.'

In today's challenging job market, you have to compete vigorously against many candidates. You have to earn each and every job offer. Sometimes you even need to convince a company to create a position that currently doesn't even exist.

Interviewers have to see more than just your smiling face. Recruitment managers must be convinced there is a reason to hire you. They have to be shown that the benefits of hiring you will far outweigh the costs of doing so. To create a position, most managers go through a similar recruiting process. I call this recruiting methodology the 7-Step Recruitment Process.

The 7-Step Recruitment Process

1 Identify a business need
2 Pinpoint potential solutions

3   Decide to recruit a new employee
4   Develop a business case to justify the recruitment
5   Create a budget for the position
6   Define the recruiting criteria and job description
7   Conduct the search for candidates.

Every recruitment manager has to go through a justification process in order to be able to hire someone for the company. Employers don't just hire people because it feels good.

There has to be a business reason or a personal need to do so. The following 7-step process is the recruitment methodology I used as a sales manager for a large technology firm. My goal in showing you this process is to provide you with insight into the mind-set and perspective of a recruitment manager. Armed with this knowledge, you'll be able to position your skills and talents to convince companies to hire you – even when no positions are currently available.

Step 1: Identify A Business Need

The first step of any recruitment process is an acknowledgement that there is a particular business challenge or personal need. This could be anything from poor customer service to sluggish sales growth to the fact that the company's computer systems keep crashing. The bottom line is that there is something that needs to be improved or fixed in order for the business to operate more profitably or effectively.

Step 2: Pinpoint Potential Solutions

Once a challenge is acknowledged, managers have to ascertain all the possible solutions for the given problem. Solutions can come in a variety of forms. Recruitment, training, refocusing and procuring are four of the most common ways to solve a problem.

Let's say a manager wants to improve customer service. Any one of the following scenarios could solve the problem. Possible customer-service solutions include:

- Install new customer service software
- Recruit more customer service representatives
- Sack the current customer service manager
- Recruit a consultant who can make recommendations
- Give unhappy customers a voucher towards future purchases
- Provide customer service training to the existing staff
- Reorganise the existing customer service department.

In this scenario you can see that even though there is one problem (poor customer service), there are at least seven possible solutions. Any one of these solutions could potentially solve the problem. It is up to the recruitment manager to determine which will be the most cost-effective and productive.

Step 3: Decide To Recruit A New Employee

As you saw in the previous example on poor customer service, there are many ways to solve a business problem. Recruiting more people may be one answer. Installing a new computer platform and training the existing staff are other potential solutions.

Managers must weigh all the alternative solutions and work out which is the most effective. They may ask others for advice as well. Ultimately, they will reach a decision. Often, this decision is to recruit someone. However, many times it is not.

When trying to convince a company to create a position for you, one key is to quantify how you can provide a better return on their investment than other possible alternatives.

Companies don't hire people just to be nice!

Companies expect to make a large return on their investment. Have you ever taken the time to work out the pounds and pence of what kind of return you can provide to a given company? Companies employ people to either contribute towards revenues and profits or to increase efficiencies.

Employees must consistently justify their existence

Regardless of the position, when employees are not contributing in some way to the company's bottom line, they will be in jeopardy of losing their job. When companies lay off people, the first to go are usually those whose jobs are the most difficult to quantify and justify. Companies also lay off those employees who aren't the best fit for the position or the team.

The bottom line is companies don't lay off employees who are critical to the ongoing success of the business. A pay cheque is not a birthright. Every day is a new day. In order to maintain employment, employees must contribute to the success of the organisation each and every day.

Step 4: Develop A Business Case To Justify The Recruitment

Once managers decide that the best way to solve a business need is to recruit someone, they put together a business case of why a position should be created. In their business cases, managers typically show how recruiting someone will impact on either productivity, revenues, cost structure or profits. Regardless of the justification, managers must demonstrate that recruiting someone will provide a large 'return on investment' (ROI) to the company.

ROI is the benefit gained for the money invested. For instance, if you are putting money into a savings account paying 5% interest, your ROI is 5%. Companies typically look for an ROI of at least 300% before they recruit an individual. This means that in order to justify recruiting someone, managers have to demonstrate that for every £1 they invest in a new employee, they will get at least £3 back in benefits to their line of business.

Employees are expensive. Not only is there the base salary, there are also benefits and training costs. Benefits alone cost a company as much as 50% of any given employee's salary.

Let's say you are interviewing for a job that is paying £100,000 plus benefits (£150,000 total). You must demonstrate how you will positively impact on a company's bottom line by at least £450,000 (£150,000 × 3). And, that doesn't even include training costs. Ideally, you want to be able to show an even greater impact because many companies have a much higher hurdle to jump than just a 300% ROI. Some are as high as 2,000%.

What kind of return can you provide to a company?

If you can't answer this question you might as well stop job hunting. I don't care if you are an administrative assistant, an accountant, a lawyer, an architect or a salesperson; if you have no idea how you can contribute to a company's bottom line, you are sunk. Focus on what you can do and the benefits you can provide. Think about the results you can generate. Try to quantify some of those results. If you are in sales, show how you can add £300,000 in revenue. If you are a purchasing assistant, show how you can save a company thousands in expenses because of your ability to negotiate. If you are a software programmer, show how you can reduce the amount of bugs in the software, saving tens of thousands of pounds in future support costs.

If you are an accountant, show how you can find tax loopholes that alone can pay for your salary.

Get the picture?

Step 5: Create A Budget For The Position

Once upper management approves the creation of a new position, recruiting managers are awarded with what is often called a 'recruiting ticket'. That gives managers the approval to go out to interview people and ultimately hire someone. However, recruiting tickets always come with stipulations and guidelines. One of these guidelines is the budget for the position. Managers are usually given a 'not to exceed' budget of how much they can offer new employees. This budget not only encompasses salary, but can also include items such as benefits, allowances and perks.

Insider Tip

Often, recruiting managers will offer something less than the maximum budget in an initial job offer. Typically, they will leave some fudge factor for negotiations.

Let's say a manager wants to hire a new computer programmer. That manager may be given a 'not to exceed' budget of £150,000 a year. As previously mentioned, often that budget includes the cost of benefits, so not all of that money can go towards salary. Benefits are typically assigned a value of anywhere from 25% to 50%. Thus, in this case, the manager can offer a an annual salary of somewhere between £100,000 and £125,000.

Insider Tip

When you are negotiating for salary, if you are married, and covered by your spouse's healthcare plan, you may be able to negotiate for more money by offering your potential employer the opportunity to forgo providing you with health insurance. This could free up additional funding for your salary for cases where healthcare is the largest component of benefit cost.

Step 6: Define The Recruiting Criteria And Job Description

Once the budget is set, recruiting managers now have to decide what kind of person to recruit. In order to do this, they will put together a list of desired qualities and characteristics. These can include the following:

- Work experience.
- Personality.
- Qualifications.
- Salary range.
- Background.
- Adaptability.
- Flexibility.
- Drive.
- Knowledge.
- Accomplishments.

Once recruiting managers determine the recruiting criteria for a given position, they will then rank the criteria by importance and relevance to the success of the position. Based on this prioritised list of criteria, managers then create a job description. Job descriptions typically include an outline of the duties of the position as well as the qualifications needed to succeed. When you see a classified ad or posting, that is the output of this step.

Insider Tip
Ideally, you want to influence a recruiting decision before this step. Typically, once managers define the job, they already have an idea of whom they want to hire. The key is to try to meet with the managers before they finalise the job description.

Step 7: Conduct The Search For Candidates

After determining the recruiting criteria and creating the job descriptions, recruiting managers are now free to initiate a candidate search. Depending on the position, managers may look at candidates inside the company, post help-wanted ads, or contact recruiters. Often, especially in more entrepreneurial firms, managers will search for candidates on their own. In larger companies, this is the time managers may finally solicit the help of the human resources department (HR).

Interesting! Notice how HR doesn't get involved until this last step. Yet how often do people focus strictly on HR during their job search? Focusing exclusively on HR is often futile because they are usually the last ones to know about a position. Managers typically already have someone in mind to recruit long before they contact HR.

When I was a manager, the only reason I had HR interview a candidate was to get a final blessing and to adhere to corporate guidelines. As a manager, I recruited scores of employees over the years. I can tell you with complete assurance that HR introduced not one of them to me.

Certainly, in some larger companies, HR can help scour the field for potential candidates. However, they rarely will make the final recruiting decision. The reason for this is that unless you are in the HR field, you will almost always be reporting to some other line of business. It is the manager, the one whom you will report to, who will make the ultimate recruiting decision.

Predict the decision-making criteria

One of the best ways to accelerate your job search is to try to predict what will be the most important criteria for your potential employers. Using these predictions, you can tailor your message – be it in your CVs, covering letters or job interviews – to kindle interest in prospective recruiting managers.

So what will go on in the minds of interviewers when they interview you? One thing for certain is the fact that they want to be as sure as possible that the person they are recruiting will solve their business needs and fit into the culture of their team and organisation. When recruiting managers interview you, there are many thoughts that go through their minds.

Typical thoughts of interviewers include:
- How quickly can this individual contribute to my group?
- How much training is this person going to require?
- Can I believe what this person is saying?
- What salary will I have to pay this person?
- Does this person have the personality to fit our culture?
- Is this person qualified?
- Will this candidate make me look good?

Interviewers want to look good

Just as you like to look good in the eyes of your bosses, your family and your friends, so recruiting managers want to look good. Will this candidate make me look good? Do interviewers really think that way when they talk to candidates? You bet they do!

Just like us, they want to look good. If it's not consciously, it's certainly subconsciously. Regardless of what anyone tells you, interviewers look out for their own self-interests first, then they consider the interests of the organisation. After all, they are only human. It's human nature to want to look out for your own self before others.

When you understand how recruiting managers think, you can best position yourself. After all, their time is valuable. Every moment they spend talking to candidates takes valuable time away from running their business segment.

In most cases, you will not be the highest priority

If you wonder why interviewers don't return your phone calls, or why they take a long time to get back to you, it is because they are busy. Managers have a business to run. While the opportunity to interview for a job may be the most important thing for you, it may not be such a high priority for them. Somehow you have to create a sense of urgency.

There are ways you can become a priority. Imagine you have a perfectly good car right now, but eventually you would like to get a fancier one with more features. How much urgency will you put on buying a new one? Maybe you'll go online to compare specifications and costs. Perhaps you will even go to a motor show or test-drive some of them. It may take you anywhere from a month to several years to make a decision, because there is no sense of urgency.

Now, imagine that your car just broke down and it's going to cost you £3,000 to fix it. On top of that, your car already has more than 125,000 miles on it. Do you think you will treat the car search with the same urgency? All of a sudden, there is a much more pressing need to do something.

The same holds true for managers. The greater their need and the more critical their problem is, the more time and energy they will spend on recruiting someone. Thus, when interviewing, you need to demonstrate not only that you solve business problems but that there is an immediate need for the company to react quickly.

Convey an image of being in demand

Just as in dating, one of the best ways to create urgency in interviewing is to show that you are in demand. Why is it that people often try much harder at the beginning of a relationship than later on? The beginning of a relationship is not exclusive and there is always that threat of being in competition with someone else. How many times, when the relationship is new, does the guy buy flowers and dinners, in contrast to later on, when the relationship is exclusive? Usually, it is a fact of life that people try harder when the stakes are higher.

Don't act desperate, even if you are

When you are in the job market, you never want to give the impression that you are exclusively dependent on any one opportunity. Instead, be confident and convey an aura that says many companies are interested in you.

It is human nature to want what is difficult to get. As much as I hate to admit it, when I dated, women always seemed to be more interested in me when I was already in a relationship than when I was completely unattached. Somehow people can just sense when you are desperate.

If interviewers are interested in you, they will react much quicker if they think you are in demand than if they think you are desperate.

Insider Tip

Play 'hard to get'. When job hunting, the best way to create that 'hard-to-get' or 'in-demand' aura is to go out and have as many interviews as possible. Even if you go on interviews for jobs that aren't ideal, when you get one job offer, it is much easier to get others.

Create a business case to justify getting hired

How do you demonstrate or quantify to a company that they will get a high return on hiring you? To do so you have to create a business case for yourself, just as managers do to justify hiring someone.

The first thing you need to do to create a business case is to equate work ethic and effort into monetary benefits. Let's say you are interviewing for an entry-level computer programming position and you are just graduating from university. How can you possibly demonstrate that the company will make a big return on their investment by recruiting you?

One way is to show how you learn quickly and work hard. Being young and energetic, you can explain how you will put in the long hours and dedication necessary to get a job done right. You can also provide examples of how efficiently you developed applications at university or college and how quickly you can solve problems. You can provide examples of how you performed well under stress, and how you were able to balance many tasks simultaneously.

In fact, you can imply how a company would have to employ two people to replace the energy, enthusiasm, hours worked and dedication that you will bring to the job.

Ah, now that's the magic nugget. A manager would have to hire two people to get the same kind of work and effort you will provide. By stating that a company would have to employ two people to get the same results, you've just doubled your ROI perception in the eyes of the interviewer.

If you have experience, quantify its value

Say you have several years of sales experience. Imagine hearing through the 'grapevine' that one of your competitors is paying its salespeople 40% more than you are making. Their salespeople are happy and making tons of money. The problem is they aren't recruiting. Should you give up? No! Instead, develop a business case.

Being a successful salesperson, assume you are currently servicing clients doing more than £3 million in business in an industry with a 28% gross margin. Well, what if you could generate the same kind of revenues for the new company? Hmm . . . £3,000,000 × 28% = £840,000. Wow! If your competitor employs you for a total package of £150,000 a year, they would make an ROI of more than 560% (£840,000/£150,000). That sounds like a good deal to me.

Create a perceived need

Just think, the £3 million in business you are currently selling is coming directly out of your competitor's potential client base. They are spending a great deal of time, money and manpower on marketing and advertising to try to lure that business from you. Imagine if your competitor could get your clients' business without having to spend all that money on marketing and advertising. Not only is the company going to gain profits, they are also increasing market share.

In addition, as the company sells more, it is going to lower its overall cost of production through efficiencies of scale. How can your competitor afford not to employ you? They need you! Amazing! You actually can create jobs where they don't exist. The key is to equate the results you can provide into monetary benefits managers can relate to and enjoy.

To create a business case you need to show:
- How you can solve their business needs
- How you can make an immediate contribution
- Why recruiting you is a better decision than any other option
- The substantial ROI you can provide
- How you will make anyone who employs you look good.

The concept of quantifying an intangible asset such as ROI can be challenging, especially if you are going for a position that isn't as easily measurable as sales, marketing, advertising or procurement. When you can't specifically quantify in monetary terms the benefits you can provide, try to focus on other things. Improved efficiency, organisation, response times, uptime and morale are all potential benefits you can provide.

You Can Win Regardless Of The Situation!

When you quantify what you can offer to an organisation and justify why you should be employed, you will succeed in getting loads of job interviews and job offers. Going through this process will provide you with the foundation you need to go out there and market yourself.

Checklist Summary
✓ Understand the recruiting process
✓ Try to predict the decision-making criteria
✓ Create a business case to justify being employed

✓ Quantify your ROI
✓ Interviewers want to look good
✓ Interviewers will hire you if they think you will solve a need and
   make them look good.

'Companies don't hire people just to be nice!'

Secret No. 5

Create Powerful CVs and Covering Letters

- Five subjects every CV should contain
- Two topics to avoid on CVs
- Three types of CV formats
- 10 laws for writing powerful CVs
- Five Cs of creating compelling covering letters

Job hunting today is very different from in the past. You used to be able to post a CV to human resources and wait by the telephone for an interview. Now, with the ever-present internet, you could be competing against literally thousands of people. In fact, I know of a person who recently advertised a position for a financial analyst, based in Chicago, on a popular internet job portal. He received more than 1,500 CVs in one day!

How can someone possibly get through 1,500 CVs? It is nearly impossible. The most an interviewer is likely to get through is 50 to 100. First, you have to be lucky to be in that first 100. Second, you have to have a message that really stands out from the crowd. The best way to change your luck is to bypass HR. However, there are many ways you can format your message so that it stands out from the crowd.

CVs And Covering Letters Must Grab Attention Fast

With today's competitive job market, it is critical to have a powerful message that grabs attention quickly. Otherwise you just won't get noticed. Believe it or not, interviewers spend only about 15–30 seconds initially reviewing a CV. If you don't catch their attention in that first 15–30 seconds, you lose!

You might think 15 seconds? That's not fair. But before you get too upset, think about how much time most products and services get to capture your attention. Have you watched television lately? If so, I am sure you have seen a trailer for a forthcoming film. How long did it run for? Film studios typically get only 30 seconds to grab your attention and to convince you to go to the cinema to see their film.

Hmm . . . 30 seconds to sell a two-hour film. How do they persuade you? Do they show you the most boring and mundane scenes? Do they show you a detailed chronology of how the movie was made? Of course not. Instead, they show you the most exciting scenes and the best lines.

CVs and covering letters are like film trailers

You get only 15–30 seconds to sell yourself when trying to get an interview. Like a trailer, the only way to grab an interviewer's immediate attention is to show your highlights. If you bore an interviewer with mundane information and job history that they aren't interested in, you won't get the job.

I have seen thousands of CVs that have been littered with useless information and contained more bullets than the Army. CVs with lots of useless and bulleted information are tough to sift through. Subsequently, it is very difficult to find the golden nuggets on why a person should be interviewed. The key is to create CVs and covering letters that highlight your 'best scenes' (strengths, competencies and quantifiable accomplishments) so interviewers want to interview you.

CVs and covering letters are your adverts

The primary purpose of CVs and covering letters is to sell your skills. You are the product being sold. To build your brand awareness, you must have a compelling message to advertise. But how do you know what you should focus on? What will generate the most interest? The best way is to imagine being in the shoes of the interviewer.

If you were looking at potential candidates for the position you are interested in, what qualities and characteristics would you look for? What expertise and quantifiable experience would you want to see?

Once you come up with the answers to those questions, you will know what to put on your CV and covering letters.

Creating CVs And Covering Letters Is Like Cooking

Regardless of what you are cooking, there are numerous ways to prepare a dish. When it comes to something such as pasta, there are literally thousands of recipes. You can have thick or thin noodles. You can prepare it with pesto sauce or with a tomato sauce. You can add vegetables or keep it plain.

It's the same thing with creating CVs and covering letters. You can take your identical information and literally swizzle it into hundreds of unique styles and formats. It really is up to your taste and what you are most comfortable with.

In this chapter, I am going to provide you with suggestions, guidelines, tools and samples that you can use to create your own recipe for great-tasting (successful) CVs and covering letters. However, just as with cooking, the best way to produce your own speciality is to try several different recipes and see which ones work best for you. First, you'll review some generic guidelines that are applicable to both CVs and covering letters. Then, we'll explore each instrument in more detail.

I must note, however, it's impossible to give you all the possible recipes for CVs and covering letters in this book. Nevertheless, I'll try to provide you with what I feel are the most important guidelines. For more information, you can find countless free recipes and ideas for CVs and covering letters on the internet. Just go to your favourite search engine and type in phrases such as 'sample CVs', 'free CV samples', 'sample covering letters', 'free sample covering letters' and 'sample CVs and covering letters'. There are also entire books dedicated simply to writing CVs and covering letters.

General Guidelines

Like most ads, the more copy (words) you have in your CVs and covering letters, the less people will remember them. Some of the most popular ads have been the simplest. One of my all-time favourite ad campaigns was Nike's 'Just do it!' It was a simple but powerful message. Nike's campaign did an excellent job of creating excitement for its products through using candid and forceful simplicity. Even though the campaign originally ran years ago, I still remember it as if it was yesterday.

For you to excel in the job hunt, you need to have a short but powerful message. Your CVs and covering letters should contain just enough information to make companies remember you and want to interview you. On any given day, human resources departments can receive hundreds, if not thousands, of CVs and covering letters.

'Your CVs and covering letters have to stand out.'

The sole purpose of the CV and covering letter is to get you the interview, not to get you hired. A powerful CV and covering letter will not land you a job, but a weak combination will cost you one!

Customise your message to each opportunity

To create a powerful message – one that will secure you an interview – you need to tailor your CVs and covering letters to each opportunity. Every job and company is different. On clothing, a label may read, 'One size fits all.' When trying to get an interview, rarely is that the case.

You have to tailor your message to the opportunity. Use your CVs and covering letters as advertisements of your success. Include information and vocabulary in your message that is appropriate for your target audience.

Use industry-specific language

If you want a job in IT, you will want to include phrases such as 'network management', 'systems optimisation', 'increased uptime' and 'relational database'. If you were seeking an accounting position, you would want to use words such as 'ledger', 'receivables', 'bottom line', 'return on investment' and 'inventories'.

It is important to convey, on your CVs and covering letters, both your experience and accomplishments, as well as your knowledge of the industry. You want to demonstrate that you have the necessary expertise.

Keep your message short but sweet

many people make the mistake of having multipage CVs, and covering letters that are full of needless information. Typically, multipage CVs and covering letters are inundated with opinions, lack the facts, and are flat-out boring! As an interviewer, I have read hundreds of CVs that literally put me to sleep. When that happened, I guarantee you – once I woke up – I immediately rejected that person and tossed it into the bin. Do you think I'm being harsh? Well, this is reality.

Convey a professional image

When you create CVs and covering letters on your computer, print them out using either a high-quality laser printer or a 'laser quality' ink jet printer. If you do not have a high-quality printer, create the CV, save it to your favourite software media, go to a local copy shop, and print your CV using their high-quality printers.

How else can you create CVs and covering letters that will get read, not thrown out? In the pages that follow, I will first show you how to create a powerful CV. Then, I'll show you how to create covering letters that will get you noticed!

Having a powerful CV is critical to any successful job hunt. When creating a CV, the most challenging tasks are determining what details to include and how to organise the information on the page. Unfortunately, there are no 'industry standards' on how to write a CV. In fact, 'job-hunting experts' typically differ in their viewpoints.

Note that I am basing this on my personal experience (both as a recruiting manager and as an adviser to many clients). Because there is no one right way of writing a CV, ultimately you have to choose what you are most comfortable with. My goal is to provide you with the information you need that will make your CV stand out from the crowd and get you interviewed.

Five Subjects Every CV Should Include

In creating a CV, there are certain main components that every CV should contain, as well as others that should be avoided. Let's first look at what should be included.

1. Profile or summary

When creating a CV, the first thing you should put on the top of the page is a one- or two-sentence description providing an overview of your personality and experience. This is the most important piece of the entire CV. If you don't capture your interviewers' attention here right away and show them that you are the most qualified candidate for the position, your CV will be tossed faster than a hot potato.

By including a few titbits about your personality and expertise, rather than an objective statement (as many suggest), you are not limiting yourself to one specific position. Instead, you are opening the door to multiple opportunities.

An opening sentence such as 'Driven, competitive, and dynamic individual known for consistently exceeding expectations . . .' is a much stronger opening to a CV than something such as 'I am interested in a position that is challenging and capitalises on my strengths and expertise.'

2. Accomplishments or achievements

The second part of your CV should include a bulleted section of quantifiable accomplishments and results. This is your personal 'highlights' section. Do you remember when I used the analogy of a film commercial that shows the best scenes and lines from the film? This is the section of your CV where you want to list your best highlights.

Nothing makes for a better highlight than a juicy, quantifiable accomplishment. Rather than hide your best stuff throughout the litany of information on your CV, it's much better to show it upfront. When the interviewer can see highlights such as 'Reduced expenses by £100,000', 'Increased customer satisfaction by 20%' and 'Increased year-over-year revenues by 35%' his or her attention will be grabbed big time.

3. Expertise or skills

The third section of your CV should include a summary of descriptions, one to three words in length, demonstrating your core expertise and experience. Depending on the job you are trying to get, you may want to further break it down into subcategories such as 'Technical Expertise' and 'Management Expertise', or 'Administrative Skills' and 'Organisational Skills'.

For this section, as well as the others, think what criteria would be important to the person who is doing the recruiting. Many times, you can get some clues from job descriptions. If an ad specifies that a company wants someone who is proficient in Microsoft Office, Excel and PowerPoint, you'd better show that expertise on your CV (assuming you have those skills).

4. Education

For this section, you want to include all the pertinent education you have received that is relevant to the job opportunities you desire. If you lack significant work-related experience you may want to expand on this section. However, those of you who have good work experience should limit this section to what is important. Unless you don't have a university or college education, putting stuff on your CV such as where you went to secondary school is not necessary. However, if you have taken some continuing education courses at a local community college or university relevant to the job you want, then that is something you might want to include. Again, think about what your potential bosses would want to see.

5. Work experience

The fifth component to your CV is the section that outlines in more detail your specific work experience. This segment is where you list the different jobs you have had and which provides objective details about your duties while in these positions.

As you will see, you can organise your information either by category or by date. The key is to include only relevant information and highlights that will make potential recruiting managers want to interview you. Relevant information should include the company or companies you worked for and any main responsibilities that demonstrate your aptitude to succeed in the job you are trying to get.

Two Topics To Avoid On CVs

You'll notice that when I discussed the five subjects every CV should contain, I left out two big ones that many 'experts' often recommend: the 'objective statement' and 'references'. Why would I suggest that? Do you have any ideas? Let's look at each one individually to understand why.

1. Objectives

Although many people recommend opening a CV with an objective statement, I am adamantly against this concept. In my mind, having a specific objective statement limits your scope of opportunities. If you start your CV with a statement such as 'A product manager position in the consumer industry' you have eliminated all the other industries and positions for which you might be qualified.

> 'Why limit the field of opportunity? It's not necessary.'

When you are too specific as to what you want, you put a lid on opportunities. You don't want to limit your possibilities by saying you are interested only in one type of job. Most companies keep CVs for at least 90 days. Often, if managers see an interesting CV, yet the candidate isn't quite the right fit for their specific opening, they will pass the CV onto someone else. It pays to not be too specific.

Starting your CV with a profile or summary instead of an objective is a great way of demonstrating your interests and abilities, without specifically stating that you will work only in one specific type of position.

2. References

Many people make the mistake of including references in their CVs. How do you know which references to include? Different interviewers will want to speak with various kinds of referees. Others may not request references at all. There is no need to volunteer the information unless you are specifically asked to do so.

Rather than including specific references on your CV, I recommend on the bottom of your CV to either include the phrase 'References available upon request' or just don't put anything at all.

Create a separate reference list

While I don't recommend putting references on your CV, I highly recommend you create a separate list of referees for those instances when you receive a request. Save it as a separate document. Then you can pick and choose from your list the referees who are most appropriate for each request.

To compile your list, try to get a combination of both work and personal references. Two or three of each is sufficient. Have accurate information for each reference including name, address, phone number, position, employer, email, and length of time you have known the referee. It is common practice to list only referees whom you have known for at least one year.

Call your references before your interviewer does

Make sure your referees are happy for you to use them. Also, be certain that they will provide a good reference. Many a good job opportunity has been lost because candidates did not contact their referees before listing them. The last thing you want is someone to be surprised by a phone call from an interviewer or recruiter and then give a negative reference.

Inform each of your referees about the type of positions you are seeking and why you feel you will succeed in those positions, so that they will be more prepared if someone calls. In fact, you may want to even prepare a 'cheat-sheet' for your referees, stating your key selling points. Also, make sure each of your referees has a copy of your most recent CV and covering letters.

Three Types Of CV Formats

There are chronological, functional and what I call 'hybrid' formats. Each format has its strengths and weaknesses. The key is to understand each one and determine the optimal format for you.

1. Chronological

A chronological CV is structured by the date(s) you were employed, starting with your most recent job. Over the years, this has been the most popular CV structure. However, just because it is the most popular doesn't necessarily mean it is the best for you.

For those who have had a strong and logical employment history, this format works perfectly. However, for others who have had large lapses of time where they were unemployed or those who want to switch industries or careers, the chronological style may not be the best format to use.

A chronological CV is constructed by listing date, job history and accomplishments. In this format, in the left-hand column, there are categories such as 'Profile', 'Accomplishments', 'Expertise', 'Work Experience' and 'Education'. On the right-hand side of the CV you fill in the details such as job description, quantifiable accomplishments and time frames of employment. What essentially makes a CV chronological is when you list your experience and accomplishments based on time, rather than on relevance.

If your most recent experience and accomplishments are the most relevant to the position you are trying to get, and you have a good work history, then the chronological format is a useful structure to adopt. However, if not, you may want to use one of the following two formats.

2. Functional

The second way you can organise your CV is by function. Here, you list your accomplishments by job description or job function instead of by date. The functional CV may be more useful if you have lapses in time where you were unemployed, or if you chose not to work. Large lapses in time can be a 'red flag' or a cause for concern to an interviewer. If this is your situation, you may be better suited with the functional approach.

With a functional CV you organise your job history according to relevance and experience, rather than by time. Instead of listing each job by the date you worked, you consolidate your experience into categories. A functional CV still contains the same core information; however, your expertise is highlighted, not your chronological history or timeline.

With the functional CV, instead of having one broad category called 'Work Experience' you might break it out into separate categories such as 'Accounting Experience' and 'Controller Experience'. This way you are putting the focus of your CV on what you have done, not on when you did it.

3. Hybrid

The third way you can structure your CV is to use a 'hybrid' layout. Hybrid incorporates the strengths of both the functional and chronological formats. You provide the information in an order of relevance to the interviewer, yet within each category you also structure the contents by date. This makes it very easy for interviewers to find the information they are most interested in, while also showing that you have had a consistent work history.

I find the hybrid format to be optimal for those who have extensive and relevant work experience. When you have had more than 10 years of experience, it's important to include only the most relevant information on your CV. It's possible a job you had eight years ago may have more relevance to a given situation than a job you did only five years ago. The hybrid format gives you the flexibility to highlight the most relevant information yet keep a logical flow.

I know some of this may sound a bit confusing, but don't worry. Towards the end of this chapter I will provide you with samples of each of the three formats of CV, using my own career as an example. Again, as I mentioned before, there is no one right format. The key is to choose the format that is right for you.

10 Laws For Writing Powerful CVs

Now that you know the subjects that every CV should contain and avoid, and the different ways you can format your CV, it's time to discuss the 10 Laws for Writing Powerful CVs.

1. Concise

In as few words as possible, make your points short and concise. Instead of saying something verbose and opinionated such as 'I am the best procurement manager that ever walked the face of the earth' state something like 'reduced procurement expenses by 15%'. Now that is short and sweet! It's also much more objective.

2. Objective and quantifiable

Nothing will turn off interviewers more than a CV beset with opinions and literary verbiage. Stick to the facts. If you were tremendously successful in eliminating wasteful spending in your previous job, then state something like 'reduced expenses by 35%'. This comes across as powerful and factual. Showing a quantifiable result such as 'reduced overhead by x%' is the best way to advertise, loud and clear, that you are a great cost-cutter.

If you are in sales, perhaps you want to convey that you are the world's greatest salesperson. Maybe you believe that you are so good you can sell sand in the desert. If so, give impressive statements like 'exceeded quota every year', 'grew year-over-year sales by over 65%' or 'won three corporate management awards'. These are powerful and factual statements.

3. Action-oriented

The best CVs contain action words. Action words bring your experience to life and get you noticed.

Action words

Achieved	Developed	Implemented
Authored	Directed	Improved
Awarded	Eliminated	Strengthened
Collaborated	Established	Supervised
Coordinated	Evaluated	Trained
Created	Featured	Utilised
Customised	Generated	Won
Demonstrated	Grew	Wrote

4. Easy to read

Often people cram so much information into their CVs that the reader has no clue where to start. Some candidates include so many bullets that the interviewer cannot possibly tell what is important. The reader should be able to find relevant and interesting information quickly.

Interviewers will spend only 15–30 seconds to initially scan your CV. If, in those 15 seconds, they cannot find what they are looking for, your CV will probably be scrunched up and tossed straight into the wastepaper basket. (Interviewers get so much practice they just hate it when they miss the basket!)

Interviewers want to quickly discover what you will bring to the job and the company. Make it easy for them to see why they should interview you and what makes you different from other candidates.

5. One or two pages

I am a big advocate of a CV being curtailed to a maximum of two pages in length. Why? Because I can't scan a CV longer than two pages in 15–30 seconds and neither can anyone else. (The only value of a multiple-page CV is that it weighs more when scrunched up, thus providing a better chance of making the wastepaper basket on the first try.)

The CV is an advertisement that creates interest in you. Your CV should create just enough curiosity for the reader to want to interview you. This can easily be accomplished in one or two pages.

The key here is to place the most recent and relevant information on the CV. Quite honestly, it typically doesn't matter what you did 15 or 20 years ago. You may even have forgotten much of that knowledge anyway. What is important to interviewers is what you have done lately.

6. Position-relevant

Many CVs are muddied with personal items that have no relevance to the reader. As a result, people often put themselves at a disadvantage before they get the chance to interview. If something personal needs to be said, say it in the interview. People have been known to include

interests, hobbies, political ideology and even religious beliefs in the
CV. This is unwise. Why give interviewers information that could get
you rejected even before the interview? Interviewers like to engage
people with interests and basic values similar to their own. If you
volunteer interests or beliefs that are different, you'll get bounced.
Why take that chance?

When you keep the information on your CV strictly business-
oriented you will have more room for what is really important:
position-relevant information. Position-relevant information (PRI) is
the information that has a significant impact in the decision-making
process for job selection. The best way to test each statement in
your CV for PRI is to ask yourself 'so what?' Put yourself in the
interviewer's shoes and, with the desired position in mind, ask
this question regarding each statement you want to include on
your CV.

Let's say you want to put on your CV 'Proficient at Microsoft
Office'. So what?

Well, if you are interviewing for a secretarial position, this could
be useful. However, if you are interviewing for a sales position selling
surgical instruments, it may be less relevant. PRI is what interviewers
care about.

Imagine being the interviewer
You can determine the appropriate PRI by putting yourself in
the position of your potential boss. Suppose you were the person
evaluating your CV. What would be important? If the position
was for product management, then an MBA, prior experience and
communication skills may be the PRI. If you are interviewing for
an engineering position or a project manager position, then the PRI
might be project history, significant outcomes and timely completion
of projects. When putting statements into your CV, ask yourself 'is
it PRI?' Does the information pass the 'so what?' test? If so, use it,
otherwise leave it out. Sometimes, by saying too much you can buy
back a sale.

7. Tells enough without telling too much

Don't tell more than you need to when creating a powerful CV. An impressive CV should contain only sensible information. The following are some of the things to avoid putting on your CV.

Don't ever put salary information on your CV

You will put yourself at a great disadvantage. It can only hurt you. If your remuneration is too high, you will be rejected without even having the chance to sell the company on why you are worth it. If your remuneration is too low, recruiting managers will not think you have the skills or confidence necessary for the job, and reject you. If you are in the ballpark, then you have placed a cap on what your job offer can be. No company will offer you more than 15–20% more than what you are currently making. Why limit your potential? There is absolutely no need to put remuneration history in your CV.

Do not list weaknesses on your CV

I know this sounds crazy but many people unknowingly list weaknesses on their CV. They then wonder why they can't get interviews. Weaknesses include jobs where you unintentionally lasted only a short time (less than three months) and any other information that could negatively reflect on you as a person. Keep the CV focused on business.

Do not give away all your best information

Save some great zingers for the interview! The CV is the advertisement that gets you the interview. Just as most people don't buy a product solely because of its ad, you will not get the job just because of your CV. However, if you have a powerful CV, you will certainly get many more interviews.

8. Incorporate feedback from others

The most important thing you can do before you distribute your CV is to proofread it. Use your word processor's spelling and grammar check. Then have others critique it. Sometimes you can get too close to your creation and miss obvious mistakes that your software does not catch.

I know in writing this book my spelling and grammar check missed several mistakes that only others could detect. The more people who critique and review your CV the better! I am always amused and amazed at how many people have mistakes in their CVs.

For example:
- Reason for leaving last job: maturity leave
- I have lurnt the Microsoft Word Computer Progrom
- Received a plague for Salesperson of the Month
- I require a salary commiserate with my extensive expertise.

Again, make sure you stick to position-relevant information. Some of the things people have included in CVs are unbelievable. Job-hunting professionals like me have seen it all.

Examples of irrelevant information

- Note: please, don't misconstrue my 10 jobs as 'job hopping', I have never left a job.
- It's best for employers that I do not work with people.
- I was working for my dad until he decided to move.
- I have a fantastic track record, although I am not a racehorse.
- I am loyal to my employer . . . feel free to respond to my CV on my office email.
- Personal interests: donating blood. Fifteen gallons so far.
- Marital status: often. Children: various.
- Reason for leaving last job: they insisted that all employees get to work by 9a.m.
- My boss made me a scapegoat, as did my three previous employers.

The bottom line is, make sure your CV contains only information that is relevant to the position. Otherwise, your CV will be a waste of paper and a waste of the interviewer's time.

9. Internet-ready

More and more companies are asking for CVs to be sent electronically (via email). Others are creating standard electronic forms that can be filled out on their websites or at kiosks in their facilities.

When a company requests that you send in a CV via email, often it is scanned for keywords. As I mentioned earlier, human resources can be inundated with thousands of CVs for any one posted opportunity. It is often physically impossible for them to wade through each and every submission.

To maximise efficiency, many firms use a computer to read CVs first. Computers decipher which CVs should be reviewed by using pre-selected criteria based on a defined subset of keywords and phrases. So, how can you create a technology-friendly CV?

Use industry and job-related 'buzzwords'

Because computers often scan CVs before humans do, it is important to use industry buzzwords or keywords on your CV. Examples of keywords for computer industry professions are 'operating system', 'network management' and 'uptime'. Examples of 'buzzwords' for legal professions are 'litigated', 'awarded' and 'negligence'.

Determine the most common phrases for your targeted industry and include them where appropriate. Action words, as mentioned earlier, are also critical, because computers will look for those as well. Believe it or not, computers can scan CVs in a very similar fashion to humans.

Create a PDF of your CV

One of the most difficult things about sending your CV online is to maintain the formatting that you intended. I have always been amazed at how the same file will look one way on one person's computer and totally different on another's.

The best way to get around this problem is to convert your CV into an Adobe PDF file format. This basically captures an image of your document exactly as it shows on your word processor: what you see is what you get. Almost everyone who uses the internet has Adobe's Acrobat Reader on their computer. If not, they can download a copy of it directly from Adobe. By having your CV in a PDF format, regardless of the type of computer or operating system the company uses, your CV can be read and printed exactly as you intended.

There are many ways you can create a PDF version of your CV. The most cost-effective is to go to Adobe's website and use the tool that converts almost any document into a PDF file. In addition, there are many places where, for a small fee, you can convert your document.

Create an unformatted, 'text-only' electronic CV

I also recommend creating a version of your CV where all you have are carriage returns, blank lines, and space bar blanks that replace tabs (text format). That way you can send an electronic CV to a company that might not have Microsoft Office or Adobe Acrobat Reader. Also, some older or more limited email systems cannot handle more than 79 characters on a line.

Granted, most companies will have the ability to receive a Word or PDF file. However, having an unformatted, electronic CV can be especially helpful when filling out forms through a company's website. This way, you can cut and paste information straight out of your CV into the form so you don't have to 'reinvent the wheel' every time.

Creating an unformatted version is very easy with most standard word processing packages. Typically, when you go to save a file, you are given an option as to what type of file. Create a different name for your text CV to prevent losing your formatted version. A name such as 'Todd_Bermont_CV' saved as a 'text-only' file makes it compatible with any email system.

Once you save a text version of your CV, then go into your operating system's notepad and open the document. Clean out any extraneous characters that were created as a result of the document being formatted in a 'text-only' format, and resave the document.

Create public versions of your CV

When most people think of job hunting as it relates to the internet, they immediately think of trying to find a position through an online portal such as Monster.com, www.fish4jobs.co.uk or www.totaljobs.com.

These sites store your information online in a database with thousands of others so that potential employers can scan them.

While in concept these portals are a fine idea, the reality is that as few as 5% of all jobs are actually found this way. Thus, I don't recommend spending more than 5% of your time focused on these sites.

With that said, if you are out of work you have nothing to lose by posting your credentials online. You never know what might happen. I am a big believer in using all the job-hunting resources available. Just be judicious with your time and spend it appropriately.

Some job sites utilise standardised forms into which they ask you to enter your information. Others allow you to post your CV as it is. The online forms can take quite a bit of time to complete. This is why I recommend you focus mainly on the 'top three'. There are many other sites you can use. But remember, if you spend more than 5% of your time filling out these forms you are probably wasting your time.

The best way to quickly fill out these standardised forms is to have your unformatted, 'text-only' CV readily available in a window on your computer screen. Often you can cut and paste parts of your internet-ready CV straight into their online forms. Also, as you are entering new information on each site, cut and paste that information into a word processing document. Most sites ask for similar information. So, by keeping the information from one site, you can save a lot of time and energy by reusing it.

In summary, not only should you have printed versions of your CV, you should also have your CV in at least one or two electronic formats that can be used for online distribution as well.

10. Attention-grabbing

As in an advertisement, your CV must look good in order to immediately grab the attention of interviewers. Ask others to read your CV and give you pointers. See if it grabs their attention. Look at your CV a day or two after you have written it to get a fresh perspective. Then, if after a few weeks you still haven't got a job, review it again. With the passing of time you often gain different ideas on how you can make improvements. I also suggest looking at other people's CVs. The best way to do this is to go to networking events and swap CVs with others.

Whether you are creating a hard copy or online CV, use a layout that is easy to read and professional. For your formatted versions, use a variety of fonts, bold face, italics and bullets to make your important points stand out. For printed CVs, use only high-quality (heavier bond) paper – not copier paper. There is something to be said for paper with a substantial feel – it conveys a good image. Use fonts such as Arial, Courier, Garamond, or Times New Roman, colours such as blue or black ink on white paper, layouts and words that create uniqueness without compromising professionalism.

For both printed and online CVs to be powerful, they need to be creative. In addition to the action words listed above, use words that express strength and confidence. For example, the phrase 'proficient at' is far stronger than 'learned'. Proficient means that not only did you learn something, you know it inside and out.

The most effective way to grab the attention and interest of interviewers is to put some of your best selling points right near the top of the CV. For years, people have unintentionally hidden their finest accomplishments in the job experience section of the CV. Sometimes, interviewers never make it that far. If you have some solid, quantifiable results or accomplishments, don't hide them. Move them to the front.

I recommend right below your personal summary, or profile (on the top of your CV), you insert a separate section called either 'achievements' or 'accomplishments'. In this section put some of your best highlights. These should strictly be your sensational, yet objective and quantifiable accomplishments. Strong statements such as 'saved £1 million in expense', 'increased productivity by 22%' and 'increased sales for XYZ by 45%' will grab the attention of interviewers and make them want to interview you.

CV Summary

A powerful CV opens the door to many interviewing opportunities. However, customising your CV for each situation can be very time-consuming. This is why covering letters exist. Covering letters are an excellent means to customise your message for each opportunity. It is much easier to change the wording of a covering letter than it is to change an entire CV. Shortly, I'll show you how to write dynamite covering letters that will command attention.

Thus far, we have discussed suggestions and guidelines on how to create a winning CV that can have the broadest possible appeal. However, if you would like more guidance and ideas, do not despair. There are many 'how-to' books dedicated to writing CVs. You can find these books in the same section of the library or bookshop where you found this book. Also, there are thousands of free and fee-based websites that can help you out. In addition, there are several computer software applications that can help you create a winning CV. Some are specific to CV generation, while others, such as word processing applications, include CV templates you can use.

Sample CVs for each format

On the following pages I have provided you with examples of CVs in the three main formats we discussed: chronological, functional and hybrid. I have also provided you with a sample chronological CV in an online, 'text-only' format.

To help better illustrate which format you should use, I have chosen to use my own career progression as an example. The chronological CV is a snapshot from earlier in my career, when I went from IBM to APC. The functional example is taken from later in my career, when I decided to leave APC. The third sample, the hybrid format, is a CV I would use now to try to get a position with another organisation. You'll notice that the more experience and accomplishments I gained, the more I move towards the hybrid format.

This is not to say that you, too, should choose a hybrid format: only you can determine what format is best for you. The key is to choose one that best fits your career accomplishments, experience and timeline. As you are looking at each sample CV, notice how I locate accomplishments right at the top of the CV to immediately grab the interviewer's attention, and how the content in each of the Five Components changes, as I progress throughout my career. This is your commercial, and you want to grab the attention of the interviewer in the first 15 seconds or less.

Finally, take note of how I use a variety of fonts, bullets and character formatting to make certain points stand out. This is your commercial, and you want to grab the attention of the interviewer in the first 15 seconds or less. I formatted these CVs with this goal in mind.

Sample Chronological CV

Todd L. Bermont
1 Main Street
Jobville
Anywhereshire
AB123 CD
Tel: +44 (0)12 3456789
tbermont@10stepjobsearch.com

Profile
Driven and results-oriented sales representative, known
for generating new business and consistently achieving
sales objectives throughout his career in selling information
technology solutions.

Accomplishments
- Won five 'Branch Manager Awards' and the 'General
  Manager's Award'
- Ranked in the 'Top 10%' of all IBM employees in 1992 NCR
  Corporation
- Sold first NCR PC solution to IL. Dept. of Public Aid
- Represented sales force in development of a new Unix
  workstation

Expertise
- Large account selling
- Territory management
- Lead generation
- Cross-selling
- Resource coordination
- Business development
- Cold-calling
- Direct-response marketing
- Negotiation
- Sales of high-tech solutions

Education
- University of Illinois, Urbana (1986) – Bachelor of Science,
  Marketing
- IBM and NCR sales education programmes

Experience

Account sales representative, IBM Corporation (1989–1992)

- Sold PS/2, AS/400, RS/6000, and consulting to a new-business, financial territory.
- More than doubled territory sales each year on quota.
- Sold the first RS/6000 minicomputer in the Chicago Finance Branch of IBM.

Territory sales representative, NCR Corporation (1986–1989)

- Sold UNIX towers and DOS personal computer solutions to an F1000 and State/Local Government, new-business territory. Chosen as the only sales representative in St Louis to provide input on a new Unix workstation under development.

References are available upon request.

Sample Functional CV

Todd L. Bermont
1 Main Street
Jobville
Anywhereshire
AB12 3CD
Tel: +44 (0)123 456789
tbermont@10stepjobsearch.com

Profile
Results-oriented and accomplished sales executive with a proven track record of achieving significant revenue growth in domestic and global F1000/OEM accounts.

Accomplishments

American Power Conversion
- Met and exceeded 100% of sales quota each and every year on quota
- Won the 1998 'Top Team Award' in North America
- Named 'Top Presenting Partner' at 1997 IBM Europe Sales Meeting
- Voted 'Top Trainer' at 1994 APC Europe Sales Meeting
- Awarded 'Top Fortune 1000 Salesperson' in 1993 IBM Corporation

IBM Corporation
- Won five 'Branch Manager Awards' and the 'General Manager's Award'
- Ranked in the 'Top 10%' of all IBM Employees in 1992 Expertise

Expertise
- Sales management
- Territory planning
- Remuneration planning
- New-business generation

- Interviewing and recruiting
- Global business strategy
- Project management
- Customer satisfaction
- People development
- Market analysis
- Product development
- Negotiation

Education
- University of Illinois, Urbana, IL (1986), Marketing, Graduated w/Honours
- IBM and NCR educational sales programmes

Sales Management Experience
- Director, OEM, American Power Conversion
- F1000 Channel Manager, American Power Conversion

In charge of managing a sales force focused on generating significant revenue growth in both new and existing strategic accounts. Responsibilities included recruiting, managing, budgeting, forecasting, funnel development, training and mentoring of salespeople. Consistently exceeded corporate objectives of increased revenue, profit and market share.

Corporate Sales Experience
- District Manager, American Power Conversion
- Account Sales Representative, IBM Corporation
- Territory Sales Representative, NCR Corporation

Sold computing solutions to F1000 and State/Local Government accounts. Developed new business and generated significant revenue growth in new and existing accounts. Consistently achieved and exceeded sales objectives.

Sample Hybrid CV

Todd L. Bermont
1 Main Street
Jobville
Anywhereshire
AB12 3CD
Tel: +44 (0)123 456789
tbermont@10stepjobsearch.com

Profile
World-renowned author, speaker and consultant known for
consistently exceeding expectations throughout his career in
coaching, sales and executive management.

Accomplishments

10 Step Corporation
- Featured: CNN, FOX, Monster.com, CareerBuilder.com,
  radio, and newspapers
- Authored three books: one ranked No. 1 'Most Popular' on
  Amazon.com
- 'National Leadership Award', Small Business Advisory
  Council
- As a lecturer at the University of Chicago, received rating of
  4.5/5.0
- Awarded 'Certificate of Merit' by Writer's Digest
- Elected to the 'Leadership Committee' at University of
  Chicago
- Developed online, job-hunting course offered by 500-plus
  colleges and universities

American Power Conversion
- Met and exceeded 100% of sales quota each and every year on
  quota
- Won the 1998 'Top Team Award' in North America

- Named 'Top Presenting Partner' at 1997 IBM Europe Sales Meeting
- Voted 'Top Trainer' at 1994 APC Europe Sales Meeting
- Awarded 'Top Fortune 1000 Salesperson' in 1993 IBM Corporation

IBM Corporation
- Won five 'Branch Manager Awards' and the 'General Manager's Award'
- Ranked in the 'Top 10%' of all IBM Employees in 1992

University of Illinois
- Graduated with Honours

Expertise
- Keynote speaking
- Career coaching
- Remuneration design
- Territory planning
- Interviewing
- Global strategy
- Project management
- Customer satisfaction
- Market analysis
- Sales training
- Sales management
- Resource coordination
- Business development
- Personnel
- Recruiting
- Product development
- Cross-selling
- Negotiation

Education
- University of Illinois, Urbana, IL (1986) – Bachelor of Science, Marketing
- Miller Heiman: Strategic Selling, Conceptual Selling & LAMP
- Acclivus – Coaching and Base Training
- Rodger Dawson – Power Negotiating
- IBM – IBM Advanced Sales School
- NCR – Sales School

Sample Text-Only CV

TODD L. BERMONT
1 Main Street
Jobville
Anywhereshire
AB12 3CD
Tel: +44 (0)123 456789
tbermont@10stepjobsearch.com

(Profile)
Driven and results-oriented sales representative, known for generating new business and consistently achieving sales objectives throughout his sales career.

(Accomplishments)

IBM
– Won Five 'Branch Manager Awards' and the 'General Manager's Award'
– Ranked in the 'Top 10%' of all IBM Employees in 1992
NCR Corporation
– Sold First NCR Personal Computer solution to the IL Dept. of Public Aid
– Chosen to represent the sales force in the development of a new Unix workstation University of Illinois
– Graduated with Honours

(Expertise)
– Large Account Selling – New Business Development – Territory Management – Cold-Calling – Lead Generation
– Direct Mailings – Cross-Selling – Negotiation – Resource Coordination – Selling IT Solutions – Selling Consulting Services – Project Management – Selling to F1000 Accounts – Selling to Government

(Education)

– University of Illinois, Urbana, IL (1986) – Bachelor of Science, Marketing
– IBM and NCR advanced selling programmes

(Work Experience)

ACCOUNT SALES REPRESENTATIVE, IBM Corporation (1989–1992) Sold PS/2, AS/400, RS/6000 and consulting to a new-business, financial territory. More than doubled territory sales each year on quota. Sold the first RS/6000 minicomputer in the Chicago Finance Branch of IBM. Won five 'Branch Manager' awards and one 'General Manager' award and was the first sales representative to bill out his own time as a consultant in the entire branch.

TERRITORY SALES REPRESENTATIVE, NCR Corporation (1986–1989)
Sold UNIX Towers and DOS Personal Computer solutions to a F1000 and State/Local Government, new-business territory. Sold first NCR PC solution to the State of Illinois Department of Public Aid. Chosen as the only sales representative in St. Louis to provide input on a new Unix workstation under development. References available upon request.

Todd L. Bermont (Page II)
Executive Management Experience

PRESIDENT, 10 Step Corporation (2000–Present)
Founded company focused on sales training, consulting and
career coaching.

Authored several books including one ranked 'most popular' in
the category by Amazon.com.

Guest lecturer at the University of Chicago's Graham School.
Instructor and developer of an online, job-hunting course
available to over 500 US colleges.

Trained and coached scores of individuals and companies on
improving productivity, enhancing selling skills and improving
results.

DIRECTOR, OEM, American Power Conversion (APC)
(1995–1999)
In charge of OEM division focused on global, strategic
partnerships with leading computer manufacturers such as
Dell, Gateway, HP, IBM and Sun. Managed more than a dozen
employees in the US and coordinated additional indirect staff
in Europe and Asia. Grew revenue more than 1,000% from 1995
to 1999 while only increasing the number of direct reports by
200%. Additional achievements included increasing attach rates,
profitability, customer satisfaction and market share.

CHANNEL MANAGER, F1000 ACCOUNTS, APC (1994–1995)
Managed a Fortune 1000 Channel, responsible for growing
the APC presence in large accounts. Key accomplishments
included more than tripling the average territory sales while
simultaneously increasing customer satisfaction and APC market
share. Contributors to this success included: revamping the
sales remuneration plan, extensive sales training, joint territory
customer calls, creation of a vertical channel support team,
development of a select major account programme and enhancing
sales tools including creating proposal and presentation databases.

Corporate Sales Experience

DISTRICT MANAGER, MIDWEST REGION, APC (1992–1994)
Sold power protection equipment to a Midwest, F1000 territory.
Increased territory revenues by more than double in 1992 and
triple in 1993. Secured the largest, single sale in the history of the
Midwest Region at that time.

ACCOUNT SALES REPRESENTATIVE, IBM Corporation
(1989–1992)
Sold PS/2, AS/400, RS/6000 and consulting to a new-business
territory. More than doubled territory sales each year on quota.
Sold the first RS/6000 minicomputer in the Chicago Finance
Branch of IBM.

TERRITORY SALES REPRESENTATIVE, NCR Corporation
(1986–1989). Sold UNIX Towers and DOS Personal Computer
solutions to a F1000, new-business territory. Sold first NCR
Personal Computers to the State of Illinois Department of Public
Aid.

References available upon request.

Five Cs Of Creating Compelling Covering Letters

Once you have created your CV, the next step is to have an outstanding covering letter that will convince interviewers to look at your CV and consider your credentials. You can have the world's most impressive CV, but if you don't have an eye-catching covering letter to go with it, don't bother sending it. The covering letter explains why you are the right candidate for a given position.

You may be thinking it's the CV's job to do that. Well, in a way yes, but the CV is more of an overview of who you are, whereas a covering letter answers the question 'Why you?' Imagine you are a product. Your CV describes what your product is; the covering letter is the salesperson who says why someone should consider purchasing.

I'm sure you've heard the saying 'You can't judge a book by its cover'. Don't believe it! The flashier and more exciting a book's cover is, the more it sells. Covering letters provide the same function for your CV that a book cover does for the contents of the book. The more interesting your covering letter, the better your chances of getting your CV read.

The covering letter is the 'tickler' advertising that encourages the reader to look at your CV. There are five Cs you should remember when creating your compelling covering letters.

1. Concise

Like the CV itself, the covering letter should be short and to the point. And like a powerful advertisement, the copy should be dazzling and grab the attention of the reader.

2. Confident

Don't be shy with your covering letters. Strut your stuff! After all, if you aren't confident in your abilities, how do you expect the interviewer to be? Your covering letter should be written in a very positive tone, conveying your confidence that you are an excellent, even the best, candidate and that you should be considered.

Like an assumptive close in selling, when you assume you will get the interview the odds are that you will. Just be careful to balance your enthusiasm. There is a very fine line between confident and cocky.

3. Customised

The main difference between the covering letter and the CV is that you add more custom tailoring to the covering letter. In the covering letter you should include references to the company you are applying to and how you will be a great asset to them. Stress how your experiences make you the best candidate for their job.

Each interviewer is going to want a different type of candidate. When you are writing your covering letters, try, once again, to put yourself in the shoes of the interviewer. Ask yourself what you would want in your ideal candidate if you were the interviewer. Then ask yourself what you can say about your career that is relevant to the opportunity at hand. That is what you should include in your covering letter.

If you are responding to a specific job posting or advertisement, make sure you make a reference to it in your covering letter. Then, as concisely and confidently as possible, state your case as to why you should be interviewed before anyone else.

4. Creative

For a covering letter to be successful, it must be creative. Think about your key selling points and how they can benefit the company or companies you are targeting. If you are a financial comptroller and you successfully reduced costs by 35% in your current job, then that may be of real interest to a company that is having trouble containing its costs.

Look at what makes you uniquely qualified. What qualities or achievements can you mention that will differentiate you from your competition and make someone want to interview you?

As you know, recruiting managers get flooded with CVs and covering letters. The ones that will stand out are those that have something unique about them. Often, it's your creativity that differentiates you from your competition.

5. Clear

A successful covering letter will always be crystal clear about the objective for the letter. In essence, your covering letter has to go for the close. What do I mean by that? In sales, going for the close means asking for the order. The objective of the covering letter is to get you an interview. Hence, be absolutely clear in your covering letter that you are the best person for the job and that you want (and expect) an interview.

Your covering letter should be concise and personalised, create interest in you, and ask for the interview. Your covering letter must also convey an understanding of the company and the opportunity, and how you will succeed in the targeted position. The key is to provide enough golden nuggets about your personality and experience that will make someone want to grant you an interview.

Following are two examples of effective covering letters. If you would like more specific guidance, there are many books written on how to generate winning covering letters. Also, as in CVs, you can find a wealth of information and sample covering letters on the internet. Just go to your favourite internet search engine and type in one of the following key phrases: 'free sample covering letters', 'sample covering letters' or 'covering letters'.

Checklist Summary

✓ CVs and covering letters are your personal advertisements.
✓ Know what to say by imagining yourself as the interviewer.
✓ There are five subjects every CV should contain.
✓ Two topics to avoid on a CV are 'objectives' and 'references'.
✓ You can format your CVs in three different ways.
✓ There are 10 laws for writing powerful CVs.
✓ Develop a separate list of references and ask permission to use them.
✓ Use the Five Cs to create compelling covering letters.
✓ Use industry 'buzzwords' that grab attention.

'You only get 15–30 seconds to sell yourself!'

Sample Covering Letter 1

Mr I. M. Hip
Head of Customer Services
Rye Bread Company
1 Interviewing Street
Jobville
Anywhereshire
AB12 3CD

Dear Mr Hip,

I am writing to apply for the position of Customer Service Manager at Rye Bread Company. Please find enclosed a copy of my CV for your information.

With my experience and background, I am confident I can make an immediate contribution to your team. Most recently, as Assistant Customer Service Manager for Baloney Industries, I helped increase customer satisfaction by 40% and reduce product returns by 33%. We were able to achieve this while simultaneously reducing headcount by more than 10%. This was accomplished through fostering teamwork, creating an innovative organisation and maximising call-routing procedures.

I would very much welcome the opportunity to meet you to discuss in more detail how my profile may be of benefit to your company.

Thank you for taking the time to consider this application.

Yours sincerely,

Vernon L. Dent

Sample Covering Letter 2

Ms Jane Interviewer
Vice President, MIS
Joe IT Company
1 Interviewing Street
Jobville
Anywhereshire
AB12 3CD

Dear Ms Interviewer,

Please find attached a copy of my CV, in application for the position of Website Developer at Joe IT Company.

With my unique ability to combine technical skills with marketing aptitude, I am confident I can make an immediate contribution to your team. Although a recent graduate of TLB University, I am not a typical new graduate. I have put myself through university by helping small businesses develop and maintain their websites. As a result, I bring a unique perspective of both current educational styles, along with real-world experience.

I should very much welcome the opportunity of meeting you to discuss further how I may be of assistance to your company. Please feel free to contact me at +44 (0)123 456 789.

Thank you for your time and consideration.

Yours sincerely,

John Q. Public

Secret No. 6

Network and Market Yourself

- Where to start
- Who to call
- Three sure-fire methods to market yourself.

The most common dilemma people encounter when faced with the daunting task of finding a new job is where to start. Unfortunately, most people start their job search by spending time on the least effective means of finding a job: Sunday's classified section and the internet.

Forget The Internet!

Do you have any idea how many people find jobs using the internet? Most studies show that as few as 5% of all jobs are found through the Web. What a pathetic number! But, think about it: if someone can post a position and in one day get more than 1,500 CVs, realistically, even if you can walk on water, what are the odds your CV will even be read, let alone get you the interview?

That is not to say the internet is useless. In fact, quite the contrary is true. The internet is a tremendous resource for finding sample CVs, interview questions and covering letters. The internet is also a fantastic tool for doing research for interviews and getting directions on how to get to them. The problem is that the internet is just not a very good tool for actually getting interviews.

If you are on a pier with 30 other fishermen, what are the odds of your catching as many fish as if you found a secret place that no one knew about? Help-wanted ads and the internet are where everyone goes to fish for a job. You won't catch many fish in those spots. Instead, find the little 'secret' places that few people know about or are willing to try.

Unfortunately, doing so requires effort. No one said this was going to be easy. Nothing worthwhile in life ever is. By virtue of the fact you have already invested in this book shows you have what it takes to succeed!

If It Seems Too Good To Be True, It Probably Is

At first the internet seemed to be the nirvana of the job hunt. What a great concept, just post a CV on the Web, respond to online help-wanted ads, and just sit there and wait for your phone to ring. I wish it were that easy.

When the internet first gained popularity and the economy was booming, it actually was a good way to get interviews. But just like the gold rush of the 1800s, by the time everyone learned of this concept, there was very little gold remaining to be mined.

Of course I am being slightly facetious in saying 'forget the internet'. I am certainly not saying you should completely ignore your internet options. Just keep in mind that if only 5% of all jobs are found through the internet, you shouldn't spend more than 5% of your time trying to find an opportunity there.

Start By Networking

Networking is the most effective means of finding a job. I know, I know, networking is such a cliché. It is probably the most overused term in the entire job-hunting vocabulary. I wish I could come up with a better term, but networking is truly the most effective way to find a job.

Studies show that somewhere between 80% and 90% of all jobs are found either through networking or personal marketing. With that being the case, common sense says that you should focus the majority of your job search on these activities.

The *Concise Oxford Dictionary* defines networking as 'interacting with others to exchange information and develop useful contacts'. In basic job-hunting terminology, networking is the act of personally contacting all your friends, relatives, previous colleagues and acquaintances to tell them you are in the job market and to actively solicit their help.

There is no better way to broadcast your message for wanting a new job. You will be amazed at the number of people you already know who may be aware of potential opportunities. If they are not, many of them will be able to give you names of people, in their companies, who may be interested in you or able to help you.

Don't Ask For A Job

Asking someone for a job is like a salesperson at a department store going up to you and asking 'May I help you?' That phrase is like hearing nails on a chalkboard.

Even if you want to be helped, we are programmed to say 'No thank you. Just looking.' When you call someone and ask for a job, the programmed response is to say 'Sorry, I can't help you.'

Don't put pressure on your friends and acquaintances by asking them for a job. Instead, describe to them the type of position you are looking for and the skills you possess. Ask them if they know of anyone to whom they can refer you. Ask them if they have any ideas on how you should approach your job hunt.

By the way, always ask people if they can help you. Yes, use the word help. Most people get a natural high from helping others. When you call someone and ask for help, instead of asking for a job outright, you are playing off of one of the positives of human nature – the desire to help. Who is going to say 'No, I don't want to help you'?

Call Everyone You Know

You never know who might know of a job opportunity. If you have held previous positions, gather all the business cards you have filed away in a drawer and start calling these people. Call your old customers or vendors. Contact all those people you've met over the years at conferences, trade shows and golf outings. Don't hesitate to call your friends and relatives either.

'There is absolutely no shame in asking someone to help you get a job. That is how the real world works and you might as well play along.'

I have found that by far the best people to network with are those whom you have had some sort of positive working relationship with in the past. If you were an advertising account executive who just got laid off, try calling people at your previous accounts and media outlets. If they liked your work, they may want to hire you internally. If you were a procurement manager, call all the vendors you used to work with. Call your old bosses as well. Several times, after I started my own business, ex-bosses have called me, unsolicited, about job openings. People rarely stay at the same company for ever anymore. One of your old bosses may be working for a different company that could use a person like you.

Former colleagues are also great people to network with. If your previous work experience is limited, that is okay, there are plenty of other sources of people you can network with. Other professionals to contact are your insurance agent, your accountant, your doctor, your dentist, and even your hairstylist or manicurist. These people talk to dozens of people every day and may know of something. University friends and acquaintances can also be excellent sources of job leads – especially those from the same area of study as you.

You have helped many of your friends and acquaintances out in the past, in part by giving them business. The least they can do is help you in your time of need. Try to provide copies of your CV to each person you contact. If you aren't comfortable giving a CV, then create a one-page summary that details some of your capabilities and accomplishments and provides guidance on why someone would want to hire you.

People Can Make Money By Helping You

Many companies offer employees cash rewards for referrals. One company I worked for gave a $500 (£350 approx) reward for referring a successful applicant. So, your friends and associates might not just be doing you a favour; they may be helping themselves.

Police departments have used bounties and rewards for centuries to get people to provide information that can help in the solving of a crime. Not surprisingly, this method is pretty effective. It can also work in the job market. I have had friends and clients in the past who have given people financial reward in exchange for help – I have known people to put out a 'bounty' of between £500 and £1,000 to anyone who provides them with a lead or information that turns into a job. I am not saying you have to do this. It is up to your comfort level and your pocket. This is just another tool you can put in your toolbox.

Church, Synagogue Or Mosque?

These organisations are a great way to network. Any given church, temple or mosque will have potentially hundreds of members who just might be able to help you out. I have found that people in a given community are very receptive to helping others out within the same community. Most religions put a large emphasis on helping others in their time of need.

Don't be afraid to approach your clergy to ask them if they know of anyone who could use your talents. Clergy have the opportunity to interface with the entire community. It is quite possible that they may know of someone who could have a job for a person like you. If you belong to a faith-based organisation, you have probably paid dues or volunteered in the past. So it is perfectly okay for you to ask your clergy for help in your time of need. That is one of the reasons faith-based organisations exist – to help the community they serve.

What other organisations have you belonged to? When you were at university, were you in societies or clubs? Did you play any sports? If so, call your former society or club members. Contact your former coaches and team-mates.

Professional Organisations Tailored To Your Needs

If you don't already belong to a group in your field of interest, it may be a good idea to join one; not just for the job hunt, but for your long-term success. Most industries have organisations tailored to their field, and you are sure to find one tailored to your needs. There are dedicated women's organisations – such as the Women's Engineering Society (www.wes.org.uk) – and organisations for people with special needs, such as RNID, which gives support and advice for people with hearing impairments (www.rnid.org.uk), or Employment

Opportunities for People with Disabilities (www.opportunities.org.uk). These are great ways to network.

Tools

Many companies have internal bulletin boards with job postings. During their lunch hour, your friends and associates can take a quick scan of the board to see if there are any openings that fit your interests.

Even better, most companies now have online databases or online bulletin boards that list open positions. In fact, one company I worked for had an 'Open Positions' database that you could search by position type and expertise. It takes only a couple of minutes for someone to scan a company's database, to see if there is anything that might be a good match for you. Also, if you have friends and contacts who are in management, they may be able to do internal networking for you with other managers in their organisation.

Many positions are in a developmental stage where funding has not yet been approved.

If your contacts are at the managerial level, they may have access to position approval databases or they may know of other counterparts who are looking for people. If you can get in before the position is posted, you may have a great chance at getting that job. At the very least, you may have an edge over future candidates.

Other Networking Resources

In recent years, several different groups have come into existence providing excellent networking opportunities for job seekers. There are many from which to choose, but a good start could be either your nearest Regional Development Agency or one of the many social networking sites such as Friends Reunited (www.friendsreunited.com) or Facebook (www.facebook.com); alternatively, for freelancers or for professionals looking for contacts in related industries you can try Linkedin (www.linkedin.com).

It is also likely you will find local networking organisations in your area. If you want help finding these organisations, go to your favourite search engine on the internet. Type in your nearest city, along with keyword phrases such as 'networking groups' or 'career transition'.

When you visit one of these networking groups or events, take several copies of your personal business cards and CVs.

Write A Script

Every person you talk to represents a potential opportunity to find a job. You never know who might be able to help you find a job. Before you start networking, write a script of what you want to say. Ideally, create a script for different circumstances. For instance, what you would say to a friend could be totally different from how you would approach your family doctor.

For your doctor you might want to say something like:

> Hello Dr Quackinbush, how are you? (Pause) I just wanted to get in touch to see if you might be able to help me on something. (Pause) Currently, I am in the process of looking for a new job as an executive assistant. I have had an excellent track record but recently was laid off. I was wondering if you had any ideas of people whom I should contact about a potential position.

Keep your script casual, yet to the point. Again, don't be afraid to call professional people to whom you have given business in the past. You have helped put food on the table for insurance agents, stockbrokers, lawyers, hairstylists, manicurists and many others. There is no shame in asking them to help you in your time of need, so that you can eat.

For friends, you could say something like:

> Amy, how are things? (Pause) Remember that fantastic job I had as personnel manager for Disco Dave's? Well, they just went bankrupt and I am now looking for a new job. I was wondering if you knew of any opportunities at your company or anyone I could contact about finding a new position? I'd really appreciate your help.

The key is you don't want to make anyone feel threatened, burdened or obliged to help. You want people to help you from the heart. I am sure you have been a good friend to many people. You have always been there when friends have needed you.

There is no shame in asking your friends to return the favour.

Surround Yourself With Positive People

When networking, it's always more comfortable to be surrounded by other people who are out of work. Let's face it, most of us like to commiserate with others from time to time. However, while it may feel good at the moment, complaining about life with others who are out of work is not the healthiest activity you can do for your job hunt. Instead, try to network with people who are upbeat and positive and, ideally, people who are employed who can help you.

Create A List Of Companies To Target

Bring several copies of that list along with several copies of your CV and business cards to your forthcoming networking events. When your contacts go through the list, they may see a name of a company at which a friend works. Now you have a great reference and starting point to use when you call into that company. Some networking forums are better than others. Don't go just for the sake of going: make sure your time is productive.

Have An Objective

Before networking, have in your mind what you want to accomplish for each activity. Set a quantifiable goal. When you go to an event with an objective such as 'I want to meet at least three people who are in my industry and get a minimum of two contact names whom I can call', you will be more focused and likely to succeed.

Insider Tip
Be willing to help others. Don't be afraid to share your advice and ideas. There is a saying that goes 'what goes around comes around'. If you are helpful to people, eventually someone will help you too.

Networking Works

As painful as networking can be, it is still by far the most effective way of scouting out job openings. The more people you meet, the greater your chances of finding an opportunity. Job hunting is a numbers game. Every person you talk to gets you that much closer to someone who has a job for you.

Market Yourself

By now, I am sure you realise that rarely do job opportunities just drop into your lap. You need to go out and earn them. Getting the job you want takes time and dedication. It also often requires doing things that aren't comfortable or natural to do.

Besides the traditional forms of networking discussed earlier in this chapter, there are three methods that you can use to go out and market yourself, so you can start landing those interviews. Some of these techniques may fit your personality, while others may not. Try them all and see what works best for you.

1. Cold-call for known job opportunities

The first method of personal marketing is making cold calls, over the telephone, for known job opportunities. A known opportunity is an actual job opportunity that you have identified either through a help-wanted ad, a posting or through networking. A cold call is calling someone, 'out of the blue', who is not expecting your call. This can be an acquaintance, friend, ex-manager or a complete stranger.

'Don't call HR!'

If you have identified companies that have a current job opening, try finding out the name of the person who would be your boss. Most people waste their time by just focusing on human resources. Well, guess what? There are many other fishermen also fishing from the human resources pier. Instead, call up the receptionist and ask for the name of the person who would be your potential boss. To get that name, think of what the most likely titles would be for your potential boss. Then call and ask the receptionist for the person who has that title. If you get a recording, just carry on until you reach a living, breathing person.

Don't be afraid to make cold calls

People can't bite you over the phone (and they rarely do in person). Call and introduce yourself. How you introduce yourself is up to you. The key is to relate to the person on the phone with some sort of common ground.

When making cold calls over the telephone, call from your home phone. Turn off the caller ID-protect feature, if you normally have your name blocked. Most companies have caller ID. If the receptionist sees your number on the caller ID he or she is more likely to answer the phone than if 'unknown' or 'private' appears on the display.

Before calling, practise your script

You will find that by having a script and practising it you will be much more comfortable making the call. Making a cold call for an interview is just like making a sales call. The best salespeople always prepare for their phone calls and meetings. If you are prepared, you will be successful. Your script should be very similar to your covering letter. Introduce yourself as concisely as possible, create interest in yourself and then close them for the interview.

Demonstrate knowledge

Include in your script hot buttons (areas of interest), and the language or lingo of the company and industry. The best place to find initial hot buttons is in company mission statements and company annual reports.

When you make your calls, try placing a mirror in front of your phone. While you are gazing at this mirror, see if you are smiling while talking. People can hear a difference in your voice if you are smiling. People can tell if you are happy, scared, insecure or somewhere in between by your tone of voice and your energy level – all of which are affected by your non-verbal expressions. Your energy level will be higher when you are smiling and your tone of voice will be more positive. People like talking to positive and energetic people, not those who seem depressed.

Example script for responding to a classified ad:

> Good morning, my name is _____ and I'm
> hoping you might be able to help me. I noticed your ad for a
> brand manager position and I was wondering if you are the
> correct person with whom to schedule an interview. (Pause for
> their answer)

If you have hit on the correct person, say something like:

> I currently work for _____company and I have an excellent
> track record in bringing new products to market. I saw your
> opportunity and immediately thought that my experience could
> be a genuine asset to your company. How would I go about
> scheduling an interview?

If not, then say something like:

> Who would you recommend I speak with about this opportunity?
> (Pause for their answer)

Getting rid of the cold-calling jitters is easy

Are you still afraid of picking up the phone and making a cold call?
You don't believe it's easy? What do you have to lose? The worst that
can happen is that the person you are calling can't help you. So what?
What is the big deal? If someone says no, are you any worse off than
before you asked for help? Of course not! It's not as if you have to
walk on hot coals. The worst that happens is that someone says 'no'.

When making cold calls, 9 out of 10 people may not be able to help
you. Don't get frustrated! Look at each individual who can't help as
getting you one step closer to a person who can. Be glad they said no.
They just got you that much closer to someone who can say yes. Don't
take rejections personally. Making cold calls is a numbers game.

There are supposed to be rejections. The more people you call, the
greater your chances are of reaching someone who might be able to
help you.

Cold-calling really works!

But you have to call the right person. When you are making cold calls, call decision-makers. Recently, a client of mine, Dave, called me because he was frustrated. He had been trying for weeks to respond to what he thought was the ideal help-wanted ad. But he wasn't having any luck. Discouraged and down, he finally called me. This was the conversation I had with Dave:

Dave: Todd, for weeks I have been calling the HR department of this company that has been advertising a sales position in my local newspaper. This job is ideal because it is only 15 minutes from my home and they want someone with the exact type of experience that I have. But, no one will return my phone calls. What should I do?

Todd: Come on Dave, you are in sales. When you call on customers, who do you try to contact?

Dave: The decision-maker, of course.

Todd: So, would you be reporting into the HR department? Would HR be your boss?

Dave: No. I would be reporting to a sales manager.

Todd: Exactly! So why are you wasting time with HR? They aren't the decision-maker, the sales manager is, right? (I paused) Why don't you call him instead?

Dave: You're right. Let me get off the phone with you and call them right away.

Indeed, just as he said, as soon as Dave got off the phone with me, he called the company's receptionist and said to her: 'I was wondering if you could tell me the name of the sales manager who covers the South Suburbs?' Without hesitation she gave him the name and transferred him directly to the sales manager. Dave then went on to say to the sales manager: 'Hello, my name is Dave and I'm your man.' The sales manager was dumbfounded. Dave went on to explain why he was calling and by the end of the phone conversation, he got the interview.

Now I am not saying that you should be so bold when you cold-call prospects. That was his personality, so it worked for him. What you should take from this story is that cold-calling can and does work. So don't be afraid to use it.

2. Cold-call for informational interviews

An informational interview is where you meet a person who can help you in your job search, but may not be in a capacity, or have an opening, to hire you. The best people to conduct informational interviews with are people at your targeted companies who are either at the same level as you would be (who can recommend you to their boss) or people who are at the level of your potential boss.

For instance, if you want a position in network administration, try contacting other network administrators who are already employed, and try calling the MIS directors or whatever the current titles are. If you would like a position in accounting, then try to meet other accountants as well as partners. If you want a job in marketing, try calling similar-level marketing professionals as well as product managers.

Typically, your counterparts at other organisations can relate to what you are going through and are usually more than happy to help you. In addition, even managers who do not have openings are often willing to meet potential candidates. Finding good people is always difficult. By talking to you now, managers have another prospect to add to their list when a position opens up.

Develop a list of prospects

Look at directories of your graduating year and social organisations you belonged to as a student. Many of these list what people are currently doing. Scan through the reports to see if anyone may be in a capacity to help you. Also, gather up all your business cards and contact files. You can use these connections when trying to line up some informational interviews as well.

Write down a list of companies that you are interested in. Then go to their websites and call their receptionists to get the names of people you should call. Finally, pick up your local phone book and come up with a list of prospects from there.

Don't meet people just for the sake of meeting people, though: focus your efforts on informational interviews with people who may be in a capacity to help you either because they are in the same industry or because they may have potential opportunities.

One more time, create a script
Once you collect a list of prospects, develop a script and start calling these people. While calling, don't put people on the spot. Just ask them if they can assist you. Tailor your script according to how you got the person's name.

If you are using a scholastic list, introduce yourself as a graduate of the university or school, or, if you are contacting a member of an organisation you belong to, introduce yourself as a fellow member.

Cold-calling an organisation to which you belong:

My name is _____ and I am graduating from _____.
The reason for my call is that I have an interest in consulting.
With the success you have enjoyed in your field, I would greatly
value your opinion. I was wondering if you might be able to
help me by giving me an honest assessment about what it takes to
succeed in your industry. (Pause) When would it be convenient
for me to meet you?

Cold-calling outside your industry:

Good afternoon, my name is _____ and I am currently a
top producer at_____ with expertise in _____. Would it
be possible if I could get your feedback for a few minutes to see
if someone of my background and skills would be a good fit in
your industry?

Cold-calling example inside your industry:

> Good morning, my name is_____ and I am currently in
> the market to change positions. I have demonstrated a consistent
> ability to reduce costs and improve productivity. I was wondering
> if you had a few moments when I could meet you and get your
> feedback on whether or not there would be a good fit for a
> person like me in your company.

Informational interviews

You never know who might be able to help you. Even though there
may be no positions open, when managers spot a great talent, they
often create a new position just to get that person into the organisation.
I have done that myself.

Once I recruited someone from a competitor, even though I didn't
have an opening, because he was a great talent and I knew he would be
a terrific addition to the team. Also, he always seemed to beat my team
when we competed with him in the field. I realised that if I couldn't
beat him, I should engage him.

If the manager can't create a position for you, he or she may refer you
to counterparts who do have openings for someone with your talents.

Prepare for informational interviews

Just like regular interviewers, the people you meet for an informational
interview also value their time. Treat them with gratitude and respect.
After all, they are going out of their way to help. Your goal for the
informational interview should be to learn as much as possible and
to identify at least one additional person who can help you. At the
beginning of the informational interview, present a brief overview
about yourself and your career objectives. Then, for the rest of the
interview, soak in as much as possible. Ask lots of questions.

Sample questions you can ask on informational interviews

- What do you enjoy most about your current position?
- What do you like least about your current job?

- What made you decide to go into this industry?
- Why did you choose to work with this company rather than others?
- What are the qualities and characteristics of successful employees?
- How much experience do you need to succeed?
- What is the best piece of advice you can give someone like me?
- Can you recommend anyone I should introduce myself to?
- Is it okay if I use your name when calling that person?

---

3. Direct response mailings

In addition to making cold calls over the phone, you can do targeted mailings to companies in your field of interest. Here you need an aggressive covering letter that clearly states your desire, your skills, your accomplishments and your credentials. As mentioned earlier, your letter has to be short, to the point and it has to generate interest in 15 seconds or less. The more creative your message is, the better off you will be. With the covering letter, include a copy of your powerful CV.

Try using special delivery or courier services
To really get the package noticed, send your information using a same-day or next-day courier service. Most executives and managers get hundreds of letters every day, and sometimes the only post that gets past the secretary or administrative assistant is a package that shows urgency: a same-day or next-day package. Priority mail from the post office also works very well and is less costly.

If you do not have the money to send by courier you can improve your chances of getting past receptionists or administrative assistants by putting a 'Personal' and/or 'Confidential' sticker on the envelope containing your credentials. You can find these at your local office supply store or at many post offices.

Faxes

Another effective way to create urgency is to send a fax to targeted companies. Here you should try to get attention without advertising to the secretary or administrative assistant that you are looking for a job.

Insider Tip

A trick I learned to get a fax by the gatekeeper is to have a cover sheet that does not mention the purpose of the fax. Then, on the final page of your fax transmission include a largely blank page that just says 'Thank you for your time'. This way your CV and covering letter will be sandwiched in the middle of the transmission and may not be as obvious to the gatekeeper.

Email

One other way for you to direct market yourself is to use email. If you are lucky, you may find the name and email address of the proper contact person on the company's website. More often than not, you will have to send your credentials to a general email address such as info@xyz.com or human.resources@xyz.com.

Email is effective because it costs you nothing, and you can blast out your CV to hundreds of companies at once. However, when you send your information to a general address it often gets deleted. Another drawback to email is that with spam and viruses becoming more and more of a problem, many people are deleting all emails they get from people they don't recognise.

Insider Tip

To get your email noticed, use a title/header that states a benefit. Put something such as 'Cost Reduction', 'Increase Your Productivity' or 'Increase Your New Business' in the title. That way it is not so obvious you are looking for a job and the person you are targeting may actually read your email. Or you can use an email header such as 'proven copywriter looking for work' or 'results-oriented management opportunity'.

Online CV 'blasts'

Another tool available to you is the online CV 'blast'. For a small fee, many services will blast your CV out to thousands of companies and/ or recruiters. Typically, the cost for such a service is about the same as the cost for two people to go out to dinner at a restaurant. But the jury is out to the effectiveness of these services.

If you have the money, my feeling is why not try it? I certainly wouldn't risk my last pound on these services, but if you can spare the cash, then by all means try one. You can find these CV-sending services either through search engines or any major job portals such as Monster.com.

Market yourself to people who need you

Don't waste your time and money sending out mailings and faxes to just anyone. Make sure you are targeted. Limit your efforts strictly towards people who may need your expertise or services.

If you are in administration, send your credentials to the director of administration or the administrative manager. If you are in sales, send the CV directly to the sales manager of your local area for that company.

To find out the names of the people you should send your credentials to, just call your targeted companies and ask. Ask who is the sales manager, administrative manager, human resources manager and so on. You will be surprised how helpful receptionists can be.

Start out by being really friendly and respectful to the receptionist. Most people treat receptionists rudely, but if you treat them with respect, they will relate to you better and want to help you more.

Be personal. Get the name of the receptionist and call that person by name. People respond much more when called by their name. Thank people very much for their assistance. You may need their help in the future, so you don't want to take them for granted.

Sample script for getting a contact name:

Good morning. May I ask whom I am speaking with? (Pause)
My name is _____ and I was wondering if you might be able

to help me. (Pause) You wouldn't happen to know the name of
the sales manager in charge of the Southern region, would you?

It is always a good practice to be cheerful and nice to everyone you
meet. You never know who might be your ticket to success.

Network And Market Yourself: Summary

In this chapter, we have discussed the importance of networking and
ways to go about doing it. Additionally, we identified three 'sure-fire
methods' you can use to sell yourself and find job opportunities. In
personal marketing, as in sales, it is impossible to close every deal.

The most successful people view each 'no' as getting that much
closer to a 'yes'. Finding interviews is just a numbers game. The more
you go out and sell yourself, the greater your chances of success. Once
you finish this book, go out there and network and market yourself.
You will be well on your way to getting the job you want.

Personal Case History: Career Overview

There is no better way to prove the effectiveness of networking and
marketing yourself than to show you my own career progression. I am
going to take you all the way back in time to when I was in secondary
school to illustrate the value of these activities.

In the following chart, you can view every job that I have had
throughout my entire career and how I found each one. In fact, out
of the 15 different jobs I have performed over the years, only one was
ever found through using either the help-wanted ads or the internet!
That was my first job, as a waiter, which wasn't the most rewarding
position I have ever held. In fact, I hated it. The only thing I learned
from it was how to make a tasty mint parfait.

I did find two other jobs through tools we will talk about in the
next chapter. However, a whopping 80% (12 out of 15) of all of the
jobs I have ever got were obtained through networking and marketing
myself. Need I say more? This stuff works!

Job	Company	How I found the job	When I got it
Busboy	Heights Banquet Hall	Help-wanted ad	Secondary School
Telemarketer	Farmers Insurance	Teacher: *Networking*	Secondary School
Salesperson	Alice in Videoland	Teacher: *Networking*	Secondary School
Salesperson	Alice in Videoland	Old Boss: *Networking*	University
Salesperson	Video King	Old Boss: *Networking*	University
Summer Intern	Royal Dutch Shell	CV Blast: *Marketing*	University
Sales Rep.	NCR Corporation	University Placement Office	Post-University
Account Mgr.	IBM Corporation	Dad's coworker: *Networking*	Post-University
District Manager	APC Corporation	Recruiter	Post-University
F1000 Manager	APC Corporation	Called VP: *Networking*	Post-University
OEM Director	APC Corporation	Called VP: *Networking*	Post-University
Guest Lecturer	University of Chicago	Religious org.: *Networking*	Post-University
Keynote Speaker	Numerous Clients	*Networking* and *Marketing*	Post-University
Sales Trainer	Numerous Clients	*Networking* and *Marketing*	Post-University
Career Coach	Numerous Clients	Speaking: *Networking*	Post-University

Checklist Summary

✓ Call everyone and anyone who can help you.
✓ There is no shame in asking for help.
✓ Don't rely on the internet to get you interviews.
✓ Cold-call for known opportunities.
✓ Cold-call for informational interviews.
✓ Proactively market yourself using blasts, faxes and mailings.
✓ Create scripts for each method of networking.
✓ More than 80% of all jobs are found by networking and marketing.

'The more you go out and market yourself the greater your chances of success.'

Secret No. 7
Utilise Available Tools and Resources

- The 10 best job-hunting tools and resources
- A complete job-search guide.

Networking and marketing your skills is tough work. At times, it's natural to feel a bit discouraged. When you get frustrated in your own efforts, don't despair: there are many other tools and resources you can use to find a job.

Do you have a toolbox in your home? What are the tools you use the most? I use my hammer and screwdriver most. In your toolbox, you probably have many more tools than just a hammer and a screwdriver. You might have a drill, a saw and a spanner. Even though you might not use those tools on a daily basis, it is still good to have them. You never know when you might need them.

In the previous chapter we talked about the two job-hunting tools you should use the most: networking and marketing. However, as with your toolbox at home, in job hunting there are many other tools at your disposal. Like your drill, saw and spanner, you probably won't use these tools on a daily basis. However, you will want to utilise them at different times throughout your job search to maximise your efforts, especially when you want to take a break from networking and making cold calls.

The 10 Best Job-Hunting Tools And Resources

In this chapter, I am going to share with you 10 of the best job-hunting tools and resources that, when all else fails, you can use to find additional job interviews. As you saw in my personal case history, there were a couple of times throughout my career where some of these tools really helped.

Top 10 tools and resources

1 Written publications
2 Online tools and resources
3 Associations
4 Trade shows
5 Recruitment agencies
6 College and university careers services
7 Chambers of commerce
8 Public events
9 Networking
10 Current and previous employers.

---

1. Written Publications

Most people typically start their job search by looking at the ads in the classified section of their local daily newspaper. However, other written publications can provide excellent leads too. Let's look at each type of publication in more detail.

Local daily newspapers

Local newspapers are excellent resources for finding job opportunities. Newspapers are especially helpful for people who want hourly and entry-level positions. On any given day, a newspaper can contain hundreds, if not thousands, of opportunities.

Higher-level positions can also be found in the classifieds when companies are rapidly expanding or relocating. When companies need to recruit a lot of people quickly, classified ads help them get the word out fast. Find out the most prominent days for help-wanted ads in your local newspaper. Usually, these ads are found in the classified or job sections of the paper.

The daily regional and business sections of your local newspapers are also excellent resources to use throughout your job hunt. You will discover many opportunities by reading stories about your area's economy. Many times you will find stories about a company expanding or relocating. When you see stories like this, get on the phone and make some calls.

If a company is building a new office or store, they may well need new employees. Don't be shy: call them. The worst that can happen is that you are told there are no openings. At least you'll have tried.

Articles about start-up businesses and new locations usually appear far sooner than the help-wanted ads themselves. If you read about a company moving to your city, be proactive. Contact them before they place help-wanted ads. This will give you an edge over your competition.

Weekly business publications

Many major cities have weekly business publications. These are great resources because they list lucrative job opportunities and provide a wealth of information about the region's local business climate. To find the weekly business publications in your area, check your local bookshops, convenience stores, newspaper stands and kiosks at train stations and bus depots, and, as always, check the internet.

National business publications

Publications such as the *Financial Times* and *The Economist* often contain at least a couple of pages of classified ads for higher-level positions, while the *Guardian*, *The Times*, the *Independent* and the *Daily Telegraph* have ads on most days. Some national business publications come out on a daily basis, while others are weekly.

Typically, the cost of advertising a position in a national periodical is much more expensive than a local newspaper. As a result, companies tend to post only their highest-level positions in national periodicals. Usually, the higher paying the position, the more difficult it is to find a qualified candidate. Because of this difficulty, companies will often resort to placing national ads to find the best talent.

I recommend subscribing to at least one or two of these national publications during your job hunt. In addition to the classified ads, they provide insights into the economy as well as new industries and businesses.

Industry publications

Most cities and regions have local publications dedicated to different industries for that area – your nearest Regional Development Agency will help you track these down. For example, the north-west of England is well served by BusinessDesk.com, which provides the region's business community with an up-to-date and accessible directory of business and professional services. Companies with targeted needs often place job advertisements in these publications. Determine what industries interest you the most and focus on the appropriate publications. In addition to local and regional publications, most industries have national and global publications as well.

Phone books

Perhaps one of the oldest yet most effective written publications still available to the job hunter is the good old-fashioned phone book. Many a job seeker has found out about an opportunity by just picking up the *Yellow Pages* and calling companies about job openings. As crude as this may sound, it can still be effective. If you know what type of company and industry you want to work in, it is very easy to get a targeted list in the phone book. This is also a good place to find some of the other resources that I will talk about in this chapter, such as recruiters and various networking organisations.

2. Online Tools And Resources

One of the earlier chapters had a very strong point: 'Forget the internet'. This was to emphasize that you shouldn't rely solely on the internet to get a job. I cannot tell you how many people have failed in their job search because all they do is sit at home and surf the internet or waste their time in chat rooms. That said, it doesn't hurt to have the internet in your job-hunting toolbox. Just remember that only about 5% of all jobs are found through the internet; so, don't spend much more than 5% of your time utilising this tool.

Company websites

One of the best ways to use the internet in your job search is to go directly to the websites of companies you are interested in. Let's say you want to get a job as a software developer. There are hundreds of thousands of companies that may need a software developer, from banks, to software companies, to manufacturers. What type of company do you want to work for?

Let's say you want to work for either a bank or an insurance company. You can go to your favourite search engine and come up with a list of potential targets. In this case, all you would need to do is type in search phrases such as 'top 50 banks', 'top 25 insurance companies' or you can get geographically specific such as 'insurance companies Manchester' or 'top banks Edinburgh'. Go to the home page of each of your target companies' websites. On most sites, companies will have a section called 'Career Seekers', 'Jobs At', 'Job Seekers', 'Human Resources' or 'Employment Opportunities'. Even during challenging times, many jobs are posted directly onto company websites. A company's internet address is usually its name, followed by an extension such as .com, .org, .biz, or .net. In the case of Dell, it is www.dell.com.

If you don't know the internet address of the company you are interested in, just go to your favourite search engine and type in the name of the company. In fact, some of these same search engines have their own sections for job openings and postings.

Use company websites to create your own opportunities

Responding to posted job opportunities is just one of the ways you can use company websites to get interviews. However, not all companies advertise open positions on the Web and not all companies will post every open position, either.

Believe it or not, you can actually use the internet to uncover opportunities that are not publicised. But how do you do that? It's easy!

Let's say you want to work in the finance department of a major manufacturer. Go directly to the website of your targeted companies. On almost every public company's website is an online version of their annual report. You can bring up that annual report and identify the 'Controller' and/or 'VP of Finance'. Then you can go to the 'contact us' section of the company's site to get the company's general phone number.

Call your potential new boss

Develop a script for what you want to say. In that script, generate interest so that person will want to talk to you. And (hint, hint) don't call and ask for a job. Instead, call, introduce yourself, and ask if you might be able to have a few minutes of that person's time to talk about improving their area of interest.

What if you want to work in some other line of business? Well, what would the title of your boss be? Go to company websites and do a search on that title. If you can't find anything, at least get the company's general phone number and make a quick phone call.

Be proactive. Rarely do even posted jobs just fall into your lap. As the famous motivational speaker Les Brown would say, 'To succeed, you have to be hungry!'

Online career portals

There are many online bulletin boards, job portals and career networks on the internet where you can electronically view job openings, post CVs and chat with other job seekers. Some of the most popular sites are Monster (www.monster.co.uk), Fish4Jobs (www.fish4jobs.co.uk), Prospects (www.prospects.ac.uk) and Workthing (www.workthing.co.uk).

In addition, there are many head hunters and job placement agencies on the internet. As always, the internet is dynamic and always changing. The best way to find online job bulletin boards and portals is to go to your favourite search engine and type in the phrase 'job search'. You'll see hundreds listed.

Just remember, there are so many of these sites that you could spend eight hours a day just surfing them. Prioritise your time and focus on the ones that are most likely to help you. Again, I don't recommend spending more than two hours a week (5% of a 40-hour workweek) on these sites.

Newspaper websites

Many local newspapers have their own websites that provide you with the ability to search online for jobs. You can search by job category and job location. Additionally, many of these newspaper websites allow you to post your CV online. Also, these sites provide recent articles and sections on job hunting that give fabulous advice.

3. Associations

Joining an association in your field of interest is a useful way to meet the 'movers and shakers' in your field. Most have monthly meetings or conference calls. Many of these organisations bring in high-powered speakers who may know of openings in your field of interest. Besides monthly meetings, most associations have member lists and job opportunity exchanges.

Depending on your field, there may be one or more organisations that you could join. The only downside is, these are sometimes costly. With that knowledge, you can learn a tremendous amount about your field of interest just by joining an association. Also, through networking, you may discover some great opportunities. Examples of associations include the Business Marketing Association, the British Medical Association, and the Confederation of Tourism, Hotel and Catering Management. By joining an association, you will learn about the latest trends and movements in your industry. Armed with this knowledge, you'll be much more articulate about your field of interest and prepared for your forthcoming interviews.

Insider Tip

If you can't afford to join an organisation, sometimes you can go to one or two meetings for free. Just say that you are considering joining their group and you may find yourself a guest at their next meeting to check it out. Most associations will let you come to at least one session for free.

4. Trade Shows

Trade shows are one of the most effective ways to leverage your time and money to find job opportunities. In one day you can meet literally dozens of people from the best companies in any given industry. You can learn much about potential employers just from what they are displaying in the booth. You will also enhance your knowledge because at trade shows you are exposed to the latest industry news. Best of all, you will be one of the only job seekers at the show.

Most industries have both local and national trade shows. Good places to start looking are the websites www.biztradeshows.com, www.businesslink.gov.uk and www.exhibitions.co.uk. These will point you to national, regional and industry-specific shows. The possibilities are endless: if you're interested in IT, for example, there's the Legal IT Show and the Travel Technology Show; of if you're more interested in the food industry, there's the IFE (the International Food and Drink Trade Exhibition), and, in the regions, The Northern Restaurant and Bar (the hospitality and trade exhibition for the north, held in Manchester) or the Taste of the West Show (held in Exeter). Trade magazines are another potential source of information about trade shows.

Prepare for every show you attend

Bring a stack of CVs with you and try to meet as many people as possible. Go to each booth and ask for someone who can give you guidance on job opportunities at their company. Leave a CV whenever possible and get a business card from everyone you meet.

After the show, call them or the people to whom they referred you and mention the show. People are much more apt to talk to a referral than to a complete stranger. You might get lucky and actually talk with someone at the show itself, someone who will engage you. You never know until you try.

Develop a script and dress appropriately

Prepare in advance what you want to say as you walk into each booth. Typically, you will have only about 30 seconds to generate interest in yourself. Be prepared and dress appropriately. If the show is a casual show, such as the motor or restaurant shows, then business casual is fine. However, if you are attending a banking show or a healthcare show, you should definitely go with business formal, as dress in these industries tends to be more conservative.

Go to shows when they are slow

Typically, at most trade shows, there are slow periods where the people working the booths don't have much to do. These are the best times to conduct your job-hunting efforts. Slow periods are usually between 8a.m. and 9a.m. or between 4p.m. and 5p.m. Other slow periods include the final hours of the last day of a show and the times when there are breakout sessions.

Insider Tip

Sometimes, going to the show during the booth setup can be advantageous. Often, trade shows do not charge an attendance fee during this time. Here you can meet the people setting up the booths. Shows can be quite expensive to get into, and admittance is often limited; so this is a way of accomplishing some of what you want to do without the cost and limitations. During setup, there are no potential customers in the booth, so people are often more willing to spend time with you.

Don't bother people at trade shows when they are busy and their booths are crowded. You don't want to interrupt them while they are conducting business. This will irritate your potential prospects and limit your chances of success. However, if you go when it is slow in the booth, people are usually much more eager to talk to you (if for no other reason than to stay awake). Sometimes, working a trade show booth can be a lonely and boring experience. During these times, people will be much more receptive to what you have to say.

5. Recruitment Agencies

Recruitment agencies are in effect an interface between buyers
and sellers, in this case between you and potential employers.
In addition to placing people for full-time employment, there
are also firms that specialise in temporary or part-time positions.
Some agencies operate nationwide, such as Manpower, others
are regional and specialist agencies. ITN Mark Education, for
example, specialises in the education sector, and Persona focuses
on south-east England.

Generally speaking, agencies receive their fees from the employer,
either through a set fee or through commission paid on the successful
placing of a candidate: an employer can pay anything from 25% to
100% of the first year's salary to the search firm. Sometimes, however,
there are fees payable by the employee, in addition. For this reason
it is important that you find the right sort of agency for your own
particular needs, and that you check very carefully all the terms and
conditions before you sign on with an agency.

Part-time positions

The opinion of many 'experts' in the field is that one of the best ways
to find a full-time job is to first work in a temporary or part-time
position. The idea is that once you prove yourself in a temporary
position, a company may see how good you are and want to engage
you for a full-time job. Additionally, the theory is that the part-time
job will help you pay your bills while you are searching for a full-time
job.

While there are indeed advantages to part-time employment, there
are also many drawbacks. First, it takes focus away from your main
objective of finding a full-time job that you really want. Second, if
you are accustomed to earning a high income, and you settle for a part-
time job for significantly less money, it can be a real blow to your ego,
which can be a significant setback to your job search.

Only you will know what is best for your situation. But if you want
to try this route, then employment agencies can be very helpful. They
can offer a wide range of jobs from the plant floor to administration,
accounting and sales. You can find these firms by looking them up

either in your local phone book or on the internet. Whether you use recruiters or agencies, make sure you are prepared.

Have your CV ready before contacting recruitment agencies

Your CV should be tailored so that recruiting agencies can market you and your skills to their clients. Often a good recruiter or agency will offer suggestions for your CV. Listen to them: they understand the type of person their client wants to recruit and the type of CV that their clients expect.

Schedule appointments with the top firms in your industry

Recruiters and agencies may have dozens of clients looking for employees just like you. However, the top industry specialists may not be located in your city. To find out who these specialists are, and where to find them, look in industry trade publications, talk with friends in the industry, and don't forget the old standby: the phone book. You can also find them on the internet by going to your favourite search engine and typing in phrases such as 'recruiter' and 'employment agency' along with the name of your home town or a nearest large city.

Develop and practise a script

A prepared script is essential because job placement professionals are busy. Typically, you will have about one minute to sell yourself. If you don't present a compelling case in the first minute, then they will just say 'We have nothing for you.' The more prepared and exciting you come across, the greater your chances of being invited to an interview.

Just as I strongly urge you not to rely solely on the internet to find a job, don't exclusively depend on recruiters or agencies either. While they tend to be a bit more effective than the Web, networking and direct marketing yourself are still the best ways to find opportunities.

6. College And University Careers Services

Another place to find out about job openings is at the careers service of the college or university you attended. Even if you graduated years ago, don't hesitate to call the careers office to see what companies are interviewing for positions. Either you or your parents paid a lot of money for your degree. Make the university do something for you. Use the potential of future donations as a carrot. Sometimes you can even get a slot on the interview schedule when companies visit campus.

If you are still at university, the careers service is a primary source of opportunities for you. Many universities allow you to submit your CV and bid for interviews. Some hold a lottery and some allow the interviewing firms to pre-select the people who will interview based on CVs (again, this emphasises the importance of a winning CV). You might also try the Graduate Recruitment Bureau, which aims to find permanent jobs for UK graduates.

7. Chambers Of Commerce

Your local chamber of commerce is another resource you can use in your job search. Here, you can find companies that are relocating to or expanding in your area. These companies hold tremendous opportunity for job seekers. People at the chamber of commerce work with local companies all the time. They just might know of an opportunity suited to you. Also, some chambers hold job-hunting events as well.

8. Public Events

There are many public events available today that offer a wealth of opportunities for job seekers. Some of these events are free. Others charge a small fee. Often these events are held at a hotel, restaurant or local convention centre.

Job fairs

Perhaps the most prevalent are events called job fairs. At a job fair, multiple companies send representatives, each searching for candidates for a wide variety of positions. Usually, job fairs are advertised in your newspaper's community or business sections and are typically sponsored by either the local newspaper or chamber of commerce. While often catering for more entry-level positions, job fairs can still be a very productive way to network, even for people with several years of experience.

9. Networking

You will find many references to networking in this book, but here I focus on those networking organisations that target specific sectors or geographic regions. One of the most successful is First Tuesday, which has been running since 1988. This is a professional networking forum for established technology entrepreneurs and companies seeking venture capital, investors and related service providers. With a current membership of 38,000 and 10 branches across Europe, First Tuesday – believe it or not – hosts meetings on the first Tuesday every month.

... Tuesday.co.uk.

... job opportunities. Here ... s from your age group, ... cision-makers, all in one ... mend either dressing in ... ng with you several copies ... y or afraid to attend these ... friendly, upbeat and a

... **yers**

... your past and present ... nding new job opportunities. ... the best opportunities for ... might be thinking, 'Come on, ... uld I want another job at the

... heir jobs not because they ... bing, but because of their boss or situation. Maybe ... he right fit anymore. Maybe the job is stale and you just need a change of pace.

If you have never before taken the time to define your ideal job, you may not be in the best job; however, you may be in the right company. You would be surprised at how much better things can be with a change in management or responsibilities. Also, if you find a job within your company, you don't forgo the holiday time you have earned and the vested time you have accumulated in your retirement plans.

One of my previous colleagues at APC left the company around the same time I did. He thought the grass was greener elsewhere. But after four years of jumping from one floundering company to another, he realised life wasn't so bad at APC after all. He had an excellent track record there, and when he contacted the company they welcomed him back. Now he has a completely different position from the one he had left four years earlier. He is rejuvenated and thrilled that he rejoined the company. You just never know.

It pays not to burn your bridges

Unfortunately, I not only burnt my bridges at times, I torched them. Getting the last word can feel good at the time, but rarely does it provide you with any long-lasting benefits. I've learned the hard way that it always pays to treat everyone with respect, regardless of how you feel. It is a small world and you never know who may hold the keys to unlocking your next opportunity.

Don't rule out your current employer

You can find out about internal job openings in human resource databases, on corporate bulletin boards, and by talking to fellow employees and managers. Sometimes, if you have a good rapport with your current managers, and they want to see you succeed, you can ask them if they know of any new job opportunities within the company.

Call your previous managers and colleagues

Rarely does someone stay at the same company for his or her entire career. If you have had good working relationships with colleagues and managers in the past, call them. It's very possible that if a previous manager liked you before, he or she may want to hire you again.

At university, I landed two summer jobs by working for previous bosses who jumped ship and went to a different company. Given the opportunity to do so, and with the knowledge of my track record, they took me on again.

Twice, since I left APC to start my own business, previous bosses have contacted me to see if I was interested in working for them at a new company. Although I cordially declined, it was nice to know those opportunities were there. So, as you can see, it is very possible that if you have been a solid performer, you may be able to find employment with a previous boss or colleague.

Checklist Summary

✓ There are 10 great resources you can use to find a job
✓ You should try every tool at your disposal – you never know where your next opportunity might be
✓ Don't forget your previous colleagues and bosses
✓ Treat everyone with respect because you never know who might hold your future keys to success.

> 'When you get frustrated, don't despair. There are many other tools and resources you can use to find a job.'

Secret No. 8

Prepare for Every Opportunity

- Learn the eight characteristics of ideal candidates
- Research prospective companies and industries
- Answer the 65 most common job-interviewing questions
- Practise, practise, practise
- Go through a final interview checklist.

Every person to whom you talk throughout your job-hunting process represents a potential opportunity. You never know who might be able to help you in your endeavours. Whether you are networking with a friend, talking to a recruiter, calling a receptionist, attending a job fair or even having a cup of coffee at a local coffee shop, be prepared.

Job opportunities can pop up at any time. Recently, I was at a local coffee shop and a woman started talking to me. She said: 'Just last week I was sitting in the very chair you are sitting in and I got a new job.' I replied: 'Really? I am actually writing a book on the topic. How did you do that?' She said: 'I sat down as I normally do, just having a cup of coffee, and I started talking to another woman. She mentioned she worked for a local school in the area. The next thing you know we started discussing my current situation and by the end of the conversation, I had a new job. I wasn't even trying – it just happened.'

You just never know who you might run into during your job search. A complete stranger might just hold the keys to your next job. It pays to prepare for any opportunity, not just your interviews. Treat each person you meet as if that person could hire you on the spot. Your dream job may just be a cup of coffee away.

In this chapter, the main focus will be to show you how to prepare for your job interviews. However, you can apply any of these principles, techniques and tips to almost any job-hunting situation that may arise, including an innocent conversation in a coffee shop.

Regardless of the opportunity, the best way to prepare is to imagine being in the shoes of the other person. If you were on the other side of a networking conversation, what would motivate you to help a person find a job? If you were the receptionist on the other end of the telephone, what could a person say that would make you want to provide assistance?

As I have suggested numerous times throughout this book, one of the best ways to prepare for any opportunity is to develop a script and practise it. No two situations will be the same, but the more you prepare and practise, the more you will know what to say and the better off you will be. For situations where you just bump into someone on the street or in a café, put together a little 30-second pitch you can use to sell yourself.

Preparing Is As Important As Playing the Game

Sports teams prepare for hours, sometimes days, watching films of the previous games of their forthcoming opponents. A football team will prepare and practise an entire week for one three-hour game. That is the kind of effort you want to bring into your job hunting. Athletes study their opponents' strengths, weaknesses and strategies. They practise how to minimise their competition's strengths while exploiting their weaknesses. They tirelessly prepare a strategy of how to win the game. To win at interviewing, you too must develop a winning strategy (prepare). Regardless of what opportunity you strive for, you are going to come up against stiff competition. The more you prepare, the better you'll be able to compete.

Insider Tip

When I interviewed candidates, the most important question I asked was 'With all of the talented candidates that I am interviewing for this position, why should I appoint you?' When answering this question, you need to show why you're better than your competition, otherwise you won't be hired.

Throughout your job search, no matter to whom you are talking, you need to be able to articulate why you should be chosen. There will always be people who have more experience. You are going to have to know how to combat that. In some cases, you may actually be accused of having too much experience. You need to be able to address that as well.

No person is perfect. Your competitors are no different. They will have weaknesses that you can exploit. Maybe someone hasn't developed as much expertise as you have. Or perhaps someone's track record isn't as good. Without being arrogant, prepare how you will convey your strengths and experience to combat any competition that may arise. In both sports and interviewing, preparation is typically the single most important factor in separating those who succeed from those who fail. Only with preparation can you reach your potential.

Blow Your Own Trumpet, But Stick To The Facts

If you don't 'toot your own horn' and sell yourself, nobody else will. As we discussed in Secret No. 4, one of the most important aspects of preparation is to articulate your strengths and competencies and bring them to life. But whatever you do, don't make things up or lie. Doing that will always come back to haunt you.

> ### Insider Tip
> My mother had a saying I still live by today: 'When you tell the truth, you never have to remember what you said.'

When I hired employees, I looked for a particular personality, competitiveness, drive and spirit. Even if a candidate had less experience, if he or she fitted the personality I desired, I was often willing to take a chance on recruiting him or her. Many times, I have taken risks believing that, in the long run, a better personality and drive will overcome any shortcomings in experience.

The first 90 seconds are the most important

Regardless of whether you are meeting a stranger for the first time, you're networking or you're interviewing, people know within the first few moments of any conversation whether they are interested in what you have to say or if they would rather watch bubbles in a fish tank. It is critical to make a powerful and lasting first impression.

The best way to create a captivating impression is to prepare for every possible job-hunting situation from meeting a stranger on the street, to networking, to making cold calls, to the interview itself, just as a sports team prepares for a championship game. One of the first steps to take in that preparation is to learn the eight characteristics of winning candidates.

The Eight Characteristics Of Winning Candidates

Companies spend tremendous sums of money conducting market research before coming out with a new product. One of the purposes of that market research is to understand what consumers want so that companies can tailor their products towards those desires. If a product doesn't contain what consumers want, nobody will buy it.

In this section, I am going to save you all the time and expense of conducting your own market research and tell you exactly what your interviewers will want. There are eight characteristics that recruiting managers expect in their ideal candidates. Just as a company has to fulfil consumer wants, so you have to give interviewers what they desire – otherwise they won't employ you.

1. Confident

Interviewers want people who are confident about themselves and their skills. If you don't feel confident and excited about yourself, then how are interviewers supposed to? Experience breeds confidence, but, if you lack experience, you can make up for it in preparation, enthusiasm and drive.

Envision going to a restaurant and asking the waiter if the fish is good. If he says 'Well, some people like it, but I've never tried it,' you may be hesitant to order the fish. However, if he says 'The fish is fantastic and it's one of our most popular dishes,' you may be more inclined to order because of the waiter's confidence about this dish.

Interviewing is very much the same. Be confident in what you are serving: yourself! Confidence instils excitement in you and in your skills. If you are excited about yourself, you will convey that enthusiasm. Everyone wants someone who is enthusiastic.

Once or twice a day, remind yourself that you are fantastic. Tell yourself that you have qualities that no other person can match. We are all human and no two people are exactly the same. So celebrate! You have something no one else has: your unique individuality. You have to believe that only you can be employed for the job. With your qualities, experience, individuality and enthusiasm, how can any company go wrong?

Most people look at life as if the glass is 'half empty' rather than 'half full'. Life is full of opportunities. I know you can have the right perspective. A positive attitude will help you not only in interviewing but also in life. Again, remember you are great. You have a tremendous amount of talent and enthusiasm. You will succeed!

2. Organised

Nothing is more annoying to interviewers than a person who is disorganised. Once again, you need to be prepared. Plan to show up early for your appointments. The quickest way to appear disorganised is to be late for an interview. That will get you rejected every time.

Before your interviews, jot down some topics you want to cover and questions you want to ask. An interview is like an open book test – you will not be thrown out of the interview for looking at your notes. Notes are perfectly acceptable. In fact, bringing notes shows forethought and preparation.

Insider Tip

One trick I use for interviews is to write (in small print on a top corner of the page) a few important notes on topics and questions to discuss along with the names of the company and people with whom I am meeting. That way, if I get nervous, I won't forget what I want to say, or to whom I am talking.

It is perfectly acceptable to take notes during the interview. If the interviewer says something important, by all means write it down. Taking notes shows your interest in the position – just do so in moderation. No one expects you to have a perfect memory. And if they do, then who wants to work for a company like that anyway? Note-taking can be useful, as long as it doesn't distract from the interview.

Besides taking notes, other things that demonstrate your organisation include how you dress, how well you can articulate your goals and objectives as well as your strengths and competencies, and the quality of your supporting materials including CVs, business cards and project portfolios, when appropriate.

3. Personable

Smile. There's an old saying that 'when you smile the whole world smiles with you'. This popular sentiment is so true. In smiling, you create a friendly atmosphere that is more pleasant for both you and the person to whom you are talking. As a result, people will be more attentive to your message. The more you smile, the more you will succeed.

Again, think of going to a restaurant. Imagine one day you have a waitress who is a grouch, and everything she does seems to be an effort. Then, another day, you have a different waitress who is cheerful and concerned about how you enjoyed your meal. Which meal would you enjoy more? To whom would you give a better tip?

Interviewing is similar. Interviewers are inundated with prospective candidates. They remember people who smile, who are genuinely pleasant, and who enjoy the interview. If you are not friendly and personable during the interview, your chances of getting the job will be slim. Who wants to work every day with a grouch? Not being friendly is the quickest way to get an interviewer to show you the door.

4. Conscientious

I have never met an interviewer who wanted to recruit someone who's work-shy. Do not, I repeat, do not go into an interview and say 'I am looking for a 9–5 job'. Forget it. Everyone wants a hard worker. Even if you don't want to work long hours, please don't say that in the interview. Interviewers want to hear that you are flexible and that you are willing to work the hours necessary to get the job done. Interviewers might ask 'Are you willing to work long hours?' To answer, you might want to say 'I am willing to spend whatever time it takes to finish the job. In some cases that might be accomplished in a normal work week, and in other cases, it might take longer.' Or interviewers could ask 'Are you looking for a straight 9–5 job?' A response to this question would be 'I am looking for a position that is challenging and best utilises my skills – more than a position that is just a 9–5 job. I'm willing to put in whatever effort it takes to succeed!' The point I am trying to get across is that employers want employees who will give 110%. You will be able to work out for yourself how long and hard you will have to work in a particular job. If the position is not for you, then you can always turn down the offer.

In today's job market, you will be competing with aggressive and motivated people who are enthusiastic and willing to work long hours. You need to convey these same traits – because, if you don't, your competitors will.

5. Efficient

In addition to wanting conscientious employees, employers want employees who will work intelligently and efficiently. Some people will take 10 hours to complete the same amount of work that others might complete in two. Employers want people who will put in a full day's work. But they do not want people who will work hard and get nothing accomplished. They want efficiency. An old saying goes 'it's better to work intelligently than to work hard'. Well, employers want it both ways. They expect you to work hard, but they also want you to work at peak productivity.

6. Creative

Whether you are interviewing for a position in marketing, accounting, computing or for a job on the plant floor, interviewers favour people who show some form of creativity. Creativity demonstrates the ability to think on your feet and dream up better methods of accomplishing objectives.

When you look at the companies that are market-leaders in their industry, typically they got there because of their creativity. They developed a better and more creative solution to a given problem, need or desire. Anyone can follow orders; however, not everyone can think above and beyond that.

You might be thinking, I'm not a creative person. Does that mean I can't get a job? No! First of all, everyone is creative in some way. Secondly, creativity is not a 'show stopper' in itself, but expressing creativity certainly helps.

Some vocations require more creativity than other ones. Creativity is more important in a position such as advertising than it is in administration. However, even in administration a boss will still prefer an employee to demonstrate some sort of creativity.

Anyone can look at a position from its job description alone. One way you can differentiate yourself and demonstrate creativity is by changing the rules of the game. Explore areas of the position to which you can add your own definitions and perspectives.

For example, let's say that you are interviewing for a claims adjuster position at an insurance company. The standard job description is that you inspect cars that were in accidents, assess the damage and negotiate a settlement with the customer. You, being the creative person you are, could demonstrate creativity by expanding the job description.

You could say something like 'Not only am I qualified to process claims, but, with my background, I can also help you streamline the process, improve customer satisfaction and save the company money.'

Super! By being creative, you have just eliminated half the people interviewing for the position. You demonstrated a talent that others did not. You showed an ability to understand and streamline processes as well as a desire to make the customer happy.

The previous candidates did not demonstrate the expertise you just stated. Now, everyone who interviews after you must articulate that they, too, have these qualities. You just 'raised the bar' on your competitors!

Even superstars have to be creative

In basketball, Michael Jordan succeeded because of his drive, tenacity and, yes, his creativity. Early in his career, he became known for his relentless attacks to the basket, his dunking skills and his power. As he got older, Michael realised the competition was starting to get wise to his moves and that he no longer had his former speed and stamina. Instead of relying on his old tactics, Michael reinvented himself by developing an incredible fade-away jump shot that was almost impossible to defend. Michael's creativity allowed him to excel against the toughest competition in basketball. As you are preparing for your opportunities, think of ways you can redefine job requirements or activities. Think of areas where you can add value that interviewers might not have thought of. But be creative without going overboard. Having a good balance will help you interview to win.

7. Goal-oriented

Today's labour force is better trained and more productive than ever before. One trait that separates the superstars from the rest of the pack is goal-orientation.

What does it mean to be goal-oriented? It means you have a reason for existence. You aren't following the pack, you are leading it. Having goals means you know what you want out of your career, your relationships and your life.

When you set goals, you know where you want to go and how to succeed. Ask the top performers in any profession and they will tell you that the main reason for their success is that they set aggressive, yet achievable, goals.

In your interviews, you will be asked questions like 'Where do you want to be in five years?' and 'What are your career aspirations?' Questions such as these differentiate one candidate from another. If you are wimpish with your answer and another candidate knows exactly what he or she wants, you lose.

It's much better to work out what you want now rather than in the pressure of the moment in a job interview. Without set goals and objectives, you will be relegated to the second team.

Do you want to go into management? Do you want to earn big money? Do you want to travel? Do you want to help others? What are your goals and aspirations? Take a few minutes now to write down a couple of ideas. Don't worry. You don't have to solve all of life just yet. You could come up with something as simple as 'I want a job where I can travel' or 'I want a position that will continue to challenge and motivate me'.

When you stop looking forward, you have no reason to live. I have known of many people who died within weeks of their retirement. Scary, huh? Why would that happen? Probably because they couldn't imagine life past their retirement. Don't let that happen to you. Life has so much to offer! Now is the time to lay the foundation for your dreams.

What makes your life a nightmare is when you fail to invest the time to dream and fail to take ownership of your happiness. By having specific goals that are aggressive and rewarding, you will not only be viewed more positively by those who are interviewing you, but you will have a much richer outlook on life.

8. Problem-solving

Companies want more from their employees than people who show up just to punch a clock. Employers expect their workers to be both doers and problem-solvers. Whether you are an assembly-line worker, a supervisor or a vice president, managers want employees who solve problems and come up with new ideas.

Some employers even offer incentive bonuses to employees who generate recommendations that save the company money. Demonstrating qualities in the interview that show you are a problem-solver will give you an edge in your interviewing. Managers want people who solve problems instead of creating them.

Thus far, we have discussed the importance of preparation for every opportunity and identified the eight characteristics interviewers want in their ideal candidates. Now, it's time to go into detail about how you can best prepare for perhaps the most important job-hunting opportunity of all: the job interview.

Four Steps To Winning Preparation: Job Interviews

For the remainder of this chapter I am going to share with you four of the best ways to prepare for your interviews. If you follow these steps, you will interview to win and get the job of your dreams.

1. Research Prospective Companies And Industries

When countries go to war, one of the first things military leaders will do is to learn about the enemy. They study their strengths, their weaknesses and their surroundings. Then they develop a plan of attack. The goal of the battle plan is simple: to win.

Many of these same principles can be applied to your job search. To win, you need to learn the strengths and weaknesses of your targeted employers and understand their surroundings (industry). Armed with this knowledge, you can develop a winning plan of attack for your job interviews and any other job-hunting opportunity that might arise.

There are multiple resources you can use to gain as much information as possible on the companies and industries in which you are interested. The more you know about the company and its industry, the better you will perform when it comes to crunch time.

Start your research by using the internet

The internet is timely, easy to use, and makes information very accessible. There are many places you can visit on the Web for free to find information that will be helpful in your research.

Company websites
Most major companies provide a wealth of information on their company websites. Typically, they provide information such as their mission statement, financial results, products and services, company history and, as mentioned before, sometimes they even post employment opportunities.

Yahoo.com
On Yahoo.com there is a link called 'Finance'. This takes you to an awesome part of the site that provides recent news and financial

information about public companies and their competition. It also offers extensive information about stock performance and analyst recommendations. They even have a message board that often provides valuable insights into the company not found anywhere else.

Vault.com

On Vault.com there is both general and financial information about most large companies. It also has a message board that employees use anonymously. Employees either vent frustrations or give compliments on this board. I have found many of these conversations on www.vault.com to be pretty accurate.

Other useful websites for tips on this area are www.ft.com, www.risk. net and www.moneyobserver.com.

There are plenty of other resources

Your local library

Here you have access to company annual reports, *Investors Chronicle*, the *Financial Times*, *Management Today*. These are all excellent resources to find information about your prospective employers.

Company receptionists and investor kits

Besides the internet and library, the company itself is a good place to find valuable information. I always find secretaries and receptionists to be extremely helpful. They usually have plenty of company information right at their fingertips. If the company is publicly traded, an even better resource is the investor relations department. Just call and ask them to send you an investor's kit. This typically contains the most recent financial reports, press releases and new product brochures, all of which provide valuable information to use in establishing rapport during the interview.

Full-service stockbrokers

If you can't get through to a company's investor relations department, then full-service brokerage houses are also fantastic places to get information. If you have an account with a full-service broker, just call him or her and ask that he or she provide you with research reports about the company interviewing you. These reports usually contain detailed information about the company's financials, products and competitors.

Company advertisements

Advertisements show how companies position themselves in the market. Some companies focus on offering the cheapest prices, while others tout their quality and customer service. Advertisements also provide valuable insights into company products, services and culture.

Newspapers and other business publications

As we discussed earlier in the book, publications such as your local newspaper and business magazines may have articles highlighting your prospective employers. Not only can you use these articles to identify job opportunities, you can also use them to come up with questions and comments for your interviews. Mentioning a recent article is often a good way to break the ice in an interview, especially if it is positive news.

One goal of research is to know more than your competitor

Whether you actually use all the previously mentioned sources of information or a small subset, the knowledge you gain will help you succeed during your interviews.

One of the keys to researching the company is to be able to position how you can help the company achieve its business goals and objectives. When you can tie together your strengths with your knowledge of the company you are interviewing with, you create a knot that will be very difficult for your competitors to untie.

Focus on what is important

With all this information in mind, what should you know and remember? Focus on company financials, products, target markets (customers), challenges, competition and industry trends. Is the company a leader in the industry? Have sales increased year to year?

Is the firm profitable? What are its best-selling products? What are the profit margins? Is the company conservative or a risk-taker? Does the company have a lot of long-term debt, or do they have cash in the bank? Are there recent government regulations or actions that may have affected the industry?

This information will be extremely useful throughout the interview and makes a great rapport builder. For instance, if you are interviewing for a position at a bank, you could start the conversation with 'How has the Bank of England's action to change the discount rate affected your deposits?' If you are interviewing for a computer company, you could ask, 'In such a highly competitive market where computers are becoming more of a commodity, how has your company continued to grow profits while others have failed?'

Every annual report has a mission statement

Companies conduct their operations and form their corporate culture according to the philosophies found in the mission statement. By showing how your skills and talents can help the company achieve their mission, you will convey the message that you will be a valuable addition to the team.

Mission statements also provide useful insights into a company's values and beliefs. You can incorporate into the interview how you complement these values. This will also help you establish rapport with interviewers.

Identify company strengths and weaknesses

When you can relate how your skills can augment a company's strengths and how your expertise can help them overcome their weaknesses, you become a much more valuable commodity.

For example, the company interviewing you may be successful because of its team approach. In this case, you could focus on how you are a great team player and how you have led teams to success in your previous job.

Conversely, a company may have weaknesses in certain areas. Perhaps they are interviewing you to eliminate one of these weaknesses. Maybe they need more expertise in selling to large accounts and you have FTSE 100 experience. Focus on how you can help them by bringing new experience and proven success to the table.

2. Answer The Most Common Job-Interviewing Questions

You have studied the company and you have convinced yourself that you are the most qualified person for this job. You are now ready for the interview – okay? No, not quite. You're only halfway through the preparation phase. The next area of preparation is to anticipate and prepare answers for the most commonly asked job-interviewing questions.

Brainstorm on all of the possible questions you think recruiting managers will ask you during your interviews. Once you have a list of possible questions, then jot down how you should answer them.

Shortly, I will share with you 65 of the most prevalent questions interviewers will ask, along with some sample answers. When you do your brainstorming session, include these questions. Then use my mock-up responses as a guide for coming up with your own answers to these questions. Tailor your answers to your strengths. After all, interviewers will be interviewing you, not me. Let's dive in!

1. 'Why are you interested in this position?'

Example:

> The job description is a perfect match for my skills and aspirations. This is a win–win opportunity. I know I can be a real asset to your company and believe that my successes will be rewarded.

This question separates the contenders from the pretenders. Here, a boss wants someone enthusiastic and who is a go-getter. If candidates answer this question without conviction, then probably they will not perform well on the job. However, if they are energetic and give a well thought-out response to the question, they are well positioned to succeed.

2. 'What are your greatest strengths?'

Example:

> One of my best strengths is that I am a team player. Whether it takes a willingness to learn or a willingness to work until 10 p.m. to complete a project, I am going to do what it takes to make the company successful.

This answer should be tailored towards the interviewer's ideal candidate. If the interviewer is looking for someone who is competitive and street-smart, then list those as key strengths. If the interviewer is looking for a team player with proven experience, then focus on those strengths.

At the beginning of every interview you should either ask 'If you had the ideal candidate for this position, what kind of qualities and characteristics would you look for?' or 'What are some of the qualities of your top performers?' By asking one of these questions early on in the interview, you will know the areas you should focus on.

3. 'What is your biggest weakness?'

Example No. 1:

> Because I am a team player, I can sometimes work too hard. There have been times when I had to step back and relax a little more.

Example No. 2:

> Being too hard on myself when I fall short of my own expectations, even though they are typically higher than what others expect of me.

This question helps interviewers determine how you will handle difficult situations. It also provides insight both into the candidate's weaknesses and integrity.

You would be amazed at how many people air dirty laundry when faced with this question. I have had people tell me their biggest weaknesses are 'dealing with pressure' or 'dealing with colleagues' – both of those are no-nos. Every job has pressures and difficult situations.

In addition, the intent of this question is to make you think and to demonstrate your ability to turn a negative into a positive. No boss likes negative feedback. The way this question is answered can tell a great deal about yourself and whether you could be a positive employee or a potential problem.

Notice how in the previous answers I turned negatives into positives for the company. I know everyone has weaknesses. I have plenty myself. But I didn't want to talk about these in the interview and neither will your interviewers want to hear about them. Instead, interviewers want to hear a positive response such as working too hard. If you demonstrate the ability to think positively, even in a negative situation, you will score valuable points in the interview.

4. 'Why do you feel you are right for this position?'

Example:

> You mentioned you are looking for someone who is motivated with a proven track record. With my tenacity and previous experience as _____, I can step in and make an immediate contribution.

This is the ultimate question for you to be able to sell yourself. If you did a good job probing into what the interviewer is looking for in the ideal candidate, you can tailor your answer, go for the close and get the offer. The interviewer expects you to be confident in answering this question and wants to be sold on you, so I recommend being assertive – even borderline aggressive – and proud of your efforts. This is where you can really snag the job.

5. 'Can you give me the highlights of your CV?'

Example:

> During my years as an accountant, I have consistently helped the company reduce expenses, make deadlines and increase efficiencies.

Many interviewers don't have time to study CVs. Sometimes they spend as little as 15–30 seconds on each. Typically, the interviewer will have seen at least 20–30 CVs before getting to yours. At this point, the interviewer's brain starts to feel as mushy as instant oatmeal.

By asking you for the highlights of your CV, the interviewer is probably admitting that he or she didn't have the time to read your CV. But that's okay. This is a great opportunity to sell your talents.

You can use the CV as an outline of your credentials. Just as overhead slides help a professional speaker stay on track during a speech, your CV can keep you focused on what it is you want to emphasise during the interview.

This question also allows you to provide editorial on the most salient points on your CV. Prepare to discuss the key items you think would be most beneficial. Be sure you translate how your key selling points will benefit the company. Only comment on those areas of your CV that are most relevant to the opportunity at hand.

6. 'Tell me about yourself.'

Example:

> I am a motivated person who always gives 110% and strives for success. I enjoy challenges. With my personality you won't have to waste a lot of time micromanaging me: I tend always to be hard on myself.

This is the ultimate cop-out question! Interviewers use this question when they are not prepared and cannot think of anything else to ask. Basically, in asking this question, interviewers are trying to work out how similar you are to them. When I interview people, I look for people who are the most similar in personality and drive to me. So in answering the question, provide information that interviewers can relate to and find interesting.

One way to stimulate the attention level of interviewers is to look at the things they have in their offices. If they have certificates and awards hanging on the walls, they are probably very confident and competitive and are looking for someone similar. People like this have egos the size of Texas. It is a good idea to stroke those egos a bit.

If they have subtle furniture and pictures of their family on their desks, they may be more down-to-earth and looking for someone with solid values and a strong work ethic. Is the office decor modern or old-fashioned? Are there fish plaques, sports trophies, or article reprints on the wall?

These kinds of things give an insight into the types of people interviewing you. People recruit candidates with similar values, viewpoints and motivations to their own.

> ‘Keep your answer to this or any question to
> 90 seconds or less!’

To answer the ‘Tell me about yourself’ question, use the first few seconds to provide some of the personal background strengths that you identified in your personal strength worksheet. Then, in the next few seconds, focus on your personal skills and experiences; in the final 20 seconds, summarise your personal attributes with your work-related strengths and relate that to a tangible benefit interviewers can digest.

7. ‘Why did you choose your university subject?’

Example:

> I chose marketing because I enjoy working with others. I have always been fascinated by how different companies position themselves and their products. Marketing allows me to capitalise on my unique blend of creativity, hard work and an ability to relate.

This is an interesting question because it gives insight into how a person thinks. Some have said 'Well, my parents were in this field, so it seemed right.' I have also heard answers such as 'I wasn't sure what I wanted, and this sounded good.' I am constantly amazed at the terrible answers I hear in response to this question.

Interviewers want someone who put thought into this decision and looked years into the future. Have a well thought-out answer to this question. Otherwise, you could knock yourself out of the running.

8. 'What are your interests?'

Example:

> I enjoy playing and watching competitive sports such as rugby, football and golf.

As a sales manager, I asked this question because I wanted people who were competitive. I looked for people who thrived on competition for their interests. Competitive individuals usually made very good salespeople. If the person played sports, I asked them if they played for fun or if they played to win. I always looked for someone who competed to win.

Other interviewers may look for totally different interests. One interest that is valued is travelling, because jobs often entail that. Even casino gambling is acceptable if the interviewer is looking for a risk-taker. The key is to be honest but share only relevant interests.

While sales managers like risk-takers, administrative managers or plant-floor managers may not. So, make sure your interests are in line with the opportunity. Like so many other questions, interviewers ask this question to see how similar you are to them.

If the interviewer has a golf-ball paperweight on the desk and a picture of Lee Westwood or Padraig Harrington on the wall and you like golf, then mention that golf is one of your passions. If the person has several pictures of family on the desk, declare how one of your interests is doing things with the family.

Answer this question in a way that demonstrates that you've got a lot in common with the person interviewing you. However, be honest!

If you don't play golf, don't say that you do. Lying in an interview will always backfire.

9. 'What are your short- and long-term goals?'

Example:

> My short-term goal is to obtain a position with a company that will challenge me and allow me to grow. One of my long-term goals is to grow with the company and move into management. I feel that in order to be a successful leader, I first have to start out in the trenches.

This question elaborates on your thought process and whether or not you are an employee who can be counted on for the long haul. If your ultimate goal is to become a doctor, but currently you are interviewing for a paralegal position, you probably won't get the job.

However, if you are interviewing to become an accountant and your short-term goal is to perfect your accounting skills while your long-term goal is to be a partner, that makes sense.

You don't have to say that you want to go into management. It is perfectly okay to say 'My long-term goal is to remain in a position where I can best contribute to the success of the company while being motivated, challenged and rewarded.' However, you'd better have a very clear idea about what you want and why you want it.

A few months ago, a potential client approached me and asked for help on her CV. Though I looked at her CV I couldn't tell from it what kind of job she wanted. So I asked her what she wanted to do for a living.

She said she wanted to go into insurance. I said 'Okay. What do you want to do in insurance?' She said, 'I am not sure . . . perhaps to process claims.' This was strange because her CV said she had just completed law school.

I said to her 'Please don't take offence, but why would you want to go into claims processing when you just spent all that money on a law degree? That job pays a fraction of what a lawyer can earn.' She replied: 'I am not sure I want to be a lawyer. I don't think I like law. I just want a job right now.'

I was incredulous. I wanted to bang my head against the wall.
I couldn't believe what I had just heard. This person just wasted all
that time and money getting a degree in a field she didn't like and in
which she didn't want to work. In reality, she had no idea what she
really wanted.

Needless to say, I tactfully told her that I couldn't help her with her
CV until she decided what she really wanted to do. I would have been
happy to help her explore her options but before I had the chance she
stormed out in tears. She left so fast that the wind she created caused
papers to fly off my table.

Was I too critical with her? Many would think so. However, I will
tell you right now: I was not. When you are in an interview, you had
better be able to articulate your goals and objectives and how your
prior experience and credentials will be of benefit for you in achieving
those goals.

If she had told me she had always wanted to process claims,
and that her law degree would be helpful in determining the legal
legitimacy of claims, that would have been a different story. Then she
could have articulated how she could help save an insurance company
thousands of pounds by being able to spot potentially fraudulent
claims. Instead, she had no idea why she got her degree and was
not interested in working out how she could use her degree to her
advantage.

Don't find yourself in this situation. Have some idea of the
direction in which you want to go. Don't expect interviewers to help
you decide on your goals and desires. Only you truly know what you
want to do.

10. 'Tell me how your friends/family would describe you.'

Example:

They would describe me as a competitive person who has a
unique ability to succeed. Whether in school, sports or on the
job, they would describe me as a person upon whom you could
always depend to give 110% and come out ahead.

This is a great way for people to describe themselves from a unique perspective. This question gives valuable insight into how candidates feel others perceive them. How you answer this question demonstrates how you truly feel about yourself.

11. 'What interested you in [chemical engineering] ?'

Example:

> I have always enjoyed the thrill of solving complex problems and discovering new solutions.

Every profession has unique and exciting facets. What motivates a chemical engineer can be totally different from what inspires a teacher or police officer. The key is for you to be able to articulate why you chose your vocation and to show passion for your choice.

Having been a sales manager, in interviews I looked for people who said that they were stimulated by money, competition and the thrill of victory. If they didn't say one or more of these things, I would not hire them. Any good salesperson is motivated by money and shouldn't be in the business if they are not.

However, if you are interviewing for a position other than sales, you may need a totally different response. If you interviewed for a nursing or teaching position and you said that money and competition motivate you, you would probably be rejected immediately. Customise your responses to the interviewer and targeted position.

12. 'Using single words, tell me your three greatest strengths and one weakness.'

Example:

> Competitive, successful, creative and workaholic.

This question forces candidates to be concise and think quickly on their feet. Again, this provides valuable insight into the mindset of the individual. This question is also a great test of your listening skills. If you answer this question with multiple-word descriptions, it signals that you did not pay attention to the question, and demonstrates that you don't listen very well.

It is my belief (and most interviewers will agree) that if someone is not a good listener, that person will not be a good employee. So if someone asks you to describe yourself using one-word adjectives, answer in single words only.

13. 'What motivates you to succeed?'

Example:

Seeing a challenge and conquering it.

Motivation is key to success for any job. If your motivation does not fit the type of motivation for which the interviewer is looking, then there is a mismatch and you'll be kindly escorted to the door. Make sure your motivation is in line with what the interviewer would expect for the job.

If the tables were turned and you were the interviewer instead of the interviewee, what kind of motivation would you expect in the ideal candidate? For a research person or a scientist a suitable motivation would be something like 'I love the thrill of solving tough problems . . . it's almost like a game to me.' What would be the proper motivation for the position you are interviewing for?

14. 'What is your ideal job?' or 'Describe your ideal job.'

Example:

My ideal job is one that utilises my talents to the fullest and allows me to grow and be rewarded as I contribute to the success of the organisation.

Here, the candidate should state aspects of the job at hand. If the candidate's concept of the ideal job does not match the job at hand, then the interviewer will think that the candidate will not work out and move on to the next interview.

When stating your ideal job, make sure you include items from the job description of the position you are interviewing for. It's hard to hit a bullseye when you can't see the dartboard. The job description gives you a good target for which to aim.

15. 'Describe traits you want in an ideal company and job.'
Example:

> I want to work for a company that does not tolerate mediocrity and one that is growing, profitable, and an industry leader – such as yours. I want a job that is challenging and where I can make an immediate contribution.

To answer this question, again, relate qualities of the company and position that you know to be true for the opportunity at hand. If there is a match, then that is great. If not, it's on to the next candidate. Use the job description for guidance and also look to the company's mission statement. The mission statement often offers valuable insights that you can use to answer this question.

16. 'What qualities do you feel are important to be successful in ____?'
Example:

> A successful customer service representative has to be resourceful, a quick thinker and a problem-solver.

Here, you want to be able to articulate what the interviewer feels is important to succeed. There are many right answers to this question. It depends on the job and the personality of the interviewer. Be truthful with yourself and your interviewer.

Believe it or not, interviewers can usually see right through fabrications. If a shy and reserved person told me the keys to success were to be outgoing and gregarious, I immediately flushed the candidate because they did not exemplify what they were saying. Don't ever lie!

17. 'What previous experience has helped you develop the skills necessary for this job?'

Example:

> On my previous job as [an administrative assistant], often I had to work with irate customers when my boss was not around. As a result, I was pushed to learn how to ease customer tension and make quick decisions to protect valuable customer relationships.

If you do not have previous position-relevant experience, then relate some other experience that could demonstrate skills necessary for the job. An example could be as far-fetched as convincing a date to go to a hockey game rather than a film. That would demonstrate selling skills. For an accounting job, you could mention how you were the treasurer for a club at university or that you handled the finances of your housing association.

When I interviewed candidates, I immediately disqualified anyone who admitted that they had no position-relevant experience and could not come up with any experiences that could somehow relate to the opportunity at hand. Good employees have to think quickly on their feet. If a candidate did not provide an answer to a question in a timely and sincere manner, I immediately rejected that person.

18. 'Give me an example of your teamwork and leadership.'

Example:

> As project leader for [a final assembly team] I held a contest to see who could come up with the best idea to improve quality. This resulted in employees providing valuable feedback and feeling they were a part of the team. Perhaps most importantly, as a result, we reduced defects by 15%.

In most positions, teamwork is critical to success. Typically, interviewers want team players. In fact, when I hired employees, I usually wanted the best of both worlds. I looked for team players yet I also wanted people who competed to win on an individual basis.

Be careful in your answers. You need to reach a delicate balance. You don't want the interviewer to think you are too dependent on others, yet you don't want them to think you are too independent or a 'wild duck' either. The key is to demonstrate that you possess both talents and that you can go with the flow.

19. 'What was your greatest challenge and how did you overcome it?'

Example:

> My greatest challenge was handling a very emotional employee. I overcame this challenge by finding out what motivated her and discovered how to channel her emotions into positive results. As it turned out, all I had to do was to simply tell her each day how much I appreciated her efforts and how valuable she was to the team. As a result, her performance substantially improved and she became one of my best employees.

This question provides insight into how tested a person has been, and what that candidate perceives to be a big challenge. It really separates the winners from the losers. Poor candidates have a tough time of thinking of a challenge and are feeble in their answers. I looked for tough and thought-provoking challenges – ones where the person had to think beyond the bounds to solve. If someone brought up a weak challenge as being a big deal, I lost interest quickly.

20. 'Have you received any special recognition?'

Example 1:

> I won an internal quality award.

Example 2:

> I've got my Gold Duke of Edinburgh's Award.

As a recruiting manager, I did not settle for mediocre people. I expected someone to have received some sort of recognition. Good employees usually strive for recognition. If not, there is something wrong.

Recognition can be anything from a Duke of Edinburgh's Award to winning a contest to receiving a plaque for raising money for a charity. If someone can demonstrate an ability to achieve recognition, that person will probably be a strong and hardworking employee.

If you have not yet been formally recognised for your efforts, then do something to gain some sort of recognition. This can be as simple as helping with a charitable function or mentoring a child. One activity I have done in the past is to call a local school district and offer to be a guest lecturer or teacher. Teaching kids is fun and rewarding.

I have developed a tremendous respect for teachers after volunteering to be a guest lecturer. Volunteering is also a great way to give back to the community.

21. 'Why should I hire you over other candidates?'

Example:

> Because of my competitiveness, proven success and unique ability to learn, I will make an immediate contribution to the continued success of your organisation. Your company already has enough risks every day – why risk recruiting someone who is less than the best? I know I will make you proud to have hired me.

When I asked this question, I wanted the person to be a bit cocky. This is where the person can really go for the close. (Because I hired for sales, I looked for people who knew how to get the order.) I also looked for them to repeat some of the traits I noted were important during the interview. That, again, showed good listening skills.

Other managers may have different 'hot-buttons'. Put yourself in the shoes of the person interviewing you. If you were the interviewer, what would you want to see in an ideal candidate? What is it about you that would cause an interviewer to want to employ you rather than someone else? What qualities and characteristics really define and differentiate you?

22. 'Do you have any questions?'

To answer this question you should ask questions that demonstrate thought and creativity. You also want to ask assumptive questions. Assumptive questions are questions that convey a message that you expect to be hired and that you expect to be a major contributor to the team.

Example 1:

How do you reward top performers?

Example 2:

Is there a cap on earnings for top performers?

Example 3:

Looking out a year from now, if you were to give me a perfect review, what will I have accomplished?

Questions like these exude confidence. These assumptive questions illustrate that you are a positive individual and demonstrate that you are confident you will get the job. Top candidates always ask at least a couple of assumptive questions.

If candidates didn't ask assumptive questions during the interview or asked ones that were not thoughtful, I usually rejected them. I expected thought-provoking questions about company strengths, employee turnover, pay rise policies and visibility for top performers.

Don't ask questions about benefits. Save that for when you get the job offer. You can ask HR those types of questions. You don't want to ask questions that say 'what's in it for me'; instead, you want to ask questions that show 'what's in it for them'.

23. 'What did you earn last year?' or 'What are your remuneration expectations?'

Both of these are very difficult questions to answer. You must be very careful. If you give too much information, you will paint yourself into a corner and limit your potential salary. To answer these questions, use either a categorical response or a 'ballpark' figure. Personally, I prefer a categorical response such as the following.

Categorical Example:

> I am confident that I will be a top performer for your company. I expect to be compensated at a level equivalent to other top performers in your organisation.

Ballpark Example:

> Last year, I was in the ballpark of the mid-100s.

Notice that in the categorical response, not only was I somewhat evasive (so I didn't limit my options), I demonstrated confidence that I expect to be a top performer. That's a much more powerful way to answer the question.

Additional Commonly Asked Questions

What follows are some additional questions you may well come up against in your interviews. There are no example answers to these questions because I want you to exercise your mind. There is an old saying that is quite appropriate here: 'If you give a man a fish, you feed him for a day. If you teach a man to fish, you feed him for a lifetime.'

Taking this into account, I want you to learn how to fish and start preparing on your own. Answer these questions positively, and with confidence. I'll give you an example to show you how.

24. 'Why are you looking to leave your current position?'

Example of a good answer:

'I am at the stage in my career where I want a job that is more challenging and rewarding.'

Example of a bad answer:

'I am leaving because I hate my boss and my company is full of losers.'

Do not provide proprietary information

Unfortunately, sometimes companies interview people from among their competitors just to gain proprietary knowledge, not because they are actually considering recruiting someone. In addition, most interviewers look negatively upon individuals who provide information that they shouldn't give.

Providing confidential information is unethical. Proprietary or confidential information can be something as simple as telling them how many shifts a factory is running to the cost of goods or the number of people in your division.

Instead of giving exact figures, try to use percentages. If you saved more than £50,000 in expenses and if that is proprietary information, then say something like 'reduced expenses by 15%'. Rather than providing specific numbers, try to focus on percentages such as 'increased sales 120% in my territory' or 'reduced the cost of production by 33%'.

General questions

25 What qualifications do you have that most suit this job?

26 What was your greatest accomplishment at _____ company?

27 How does your company compete against ours?

28 Have you ever been asked to do something unethical? If so, how did you handle it?

29 What would your last boss say were the areas that you needed to improve upon the most?

30 What de-motivates you or discourages you?

31 What is your definition of success?

32 What was your biggest disappointment?

33 What do you feel it takes to have a successful career?

34 What do you like the most about your current position?

35 What do you like least about your current position?

36 What is the toughest decision you have ever made? Tell me about it.

37 Can you explain why you were not employed during _____ period of time?

38 Why did you choose to go into _____ industry?

39 Why did you choose to work for _____ company?

40 Is there ever a business situation where it is okay to lie about something?

41 Are you willing to accept a lower salary?

42 Why would someone with your knowledge and expertise want to interview for this job opportunity?

Leadership questions

43 When in a group setting, what is your typical role?

44 Have you ever had to sack anyone? What caused you to take this action? How did you handle it?

45 Have you ever held a leadership role? How did you motivate people to succeed in that role?

46 What was your most difficult situation? What did you learn from it?

Teamwork questions

47 How do you feel about working in a team environment?

48 Can you describe how you helped the morale of the team and motivated them to succeed?

49 Have you been in team situations where not everyone carried their fair share of the workload? If so, how did you handle the situation?

50 How would you handle a situation where the boss asked you to do something that you did not agree with?

51 Which do you enjoy more: working as a part of a team or by yourself?

Problem-solving questions

52 Can you give me an example of a difficult work situation and how you handled it?

53 How do you prioritise when you are given too many tasks to accomplish?

54 Can you give me an example of a time when you had to conform to a policy you didn't like? How did you handle it?

55 Can you tell me about a time when you went above and beyond the call of duty to get a job done?

56 Why are manhole covers round?

I know this question sounds crazy, but one of my previous managers always used to ask it. Later in this book I will tell you how to handle this question, but, first, try it on your own.

Drive and motivational questions

57 Tell me about one of your most significant accomplishments.

58 What was your favourite job and why?

59 What have you done to make yourself more proficient in X?

60 Can you give me an example of when you showed initiative?

61 Can you give me an example of a time when you motivated others to succeed?

Organisational and strategic questions

62 Do you set goals for yourself? How often?

63 Tell me about an important goal you set for yourself and how you accomplished it.

64 How do you start your workday?

65 What do you want to do in five years? Ten years?

Now comes the fun part

You need to answer each of these questions in your own words, along with any other questions you might have come up with in your brainstorming session. I have given you examples and techniques to answer these questions. Tailor your answers to your areas of interest, to your personality and to your strengths.

The questions I shared with you are based on my own personal and real-life experience. They are either questions I have been asked myself or questions I liked to ask when I interviewed people. Your own experience may differ, but these questions will give you a great head start in your preparation for winning job interviews.

Questions will vary from interviewer to interviewer, industry to industry, and company to company. But I guarantee that you will hear at least some of these questions in your next interview.

When you write down answers to these questions, I suggest that you jot down a couple of keywords that will help you remember how to respond to each enquiry. Finally, if you want even more potential interview questions, once again go to your favourite search engine on the Web. Type in search phrases such as 'free sample job interview questions', 'sample interview questions' and 'job interview questions'.

Preparing in advance

Preparing in advance will help you in almost any situation, be it interviews, networking or making cold calls. So, spend a few moments taking another look at the questions I provided. Answer them as if you were in an interview. Mould the answers to your skills, experience and personality. And, if you haven't already done so, take the time to come up with some additional questions and answers on your own.

Adapt your answers to any situation. People hire people candidates whom they like and those like them. You want interviewers to be able to relate to you on both a professional and personal level. That is why it is so important to develop a strong rapport with interviewers. By having flexibility in your answers, you are better able to relate to anyone you meet and interviewers will be much more inclined to offer you a job.

3. Practise, Practise, Practise!

There's an old story about a tourist who asks a stranger on the street 'What's the best way to get to Carnegie Hall?'

The stranger answers 'Practise, practise, practise'. At this point you may be feeling a bit overwhelmed. I know that seeing all these questions can be somewhat intimidating. But you will be surprised at how easy it is to prepare once you just dive in and do it.

The more prepared you are, the more confident you will be, and the better you will perform in the interview. However, before I leave this topic, I cannot neglect to mention the most crucial part of preparation – practice.

Role-play with your friends

Ask your friends to play the role of potential interviewers. Do not use your family, since they will be too easy on you. You want the role player to be someone who will not hesitate to provide objective feedback and criticism when necessary.

Give the role player the list of possible job-interviewing questions. To simulate spontaneity, you can write down questions on index cards and put them in a large bowl. You can then get the person playing the role of the interviewer to randomly pick questions out of the bowl to ask you.

When practising, act out the interview as if it were for real. Afterwards, get feedback. Tell your friend not to be afraid of being critical: better you're a wash-out with your friend than the interviewer!

Practise the interview until you are confident you can get the job. Start the role play by knocking on the door and entering the room. Do not break out of your role – this will impair your concentration and will not properly simulate the interview. After the interview, you can discuss how you performed. But try to complete the simulated interview first.

Record your performance

Another great way to review your practice is to record yourself using audio or video. By listening to yourself on audio or viewing yourself on video, you can really identify your strengths and weaknesses. Maybe you say the word 'um' once every 10 words. If you have a video, you might notice poor posture or a bad habit such as wiping your brow or scratching your nose.

By recognising a weakness in practice, you can work to overcome that weakness before the interview. The more you practise and prepare, the better you will do in the interview.

One final note: you can never practise too much. Professional golfers will hit buckets of balls every day to continue to improve and perfect their skills. In fact, I have heard that many golf professionals practise even after finishing a tournament. Work on perfecting your skills daily. This can be done even as you are driving your car. Talk out loud to yourself and practise your answers. You will be amazed at how this will sharpen your skills.

Try practising with a mirror

One of the ways that I have practised for my television interviews is to stand in front of a mirror and pretend that the mirror is the person interviewing me. By looking in the mirror, I can work on my smile, posture, attitude and appearance. It is amazing how much I learned about myself in doing this exercise. Try practising in front of a mirror and watch how your skills improve.

4. Review A Final Interview Checklist

Okay, now you are thoroughly prepared for the interview. You have researched the company, perfected your answers to possible questions, and you have practised. You are almost there. But there are a few final things you need to do to be prepared for your job-hunting endeavours.

✓ Get the correct spelling and pronunciation

Before any interview, know how each interviewer spells his or her name, and how the name is pronounced. Correct spelling is imperative for thank-you notes. Proper pronunciation is essential to having winning interviews. Do you like it when someone mispronounces your name? It's a sign of disrespect. Interviewers don't like it, either.

If you are not sure how a name is pronounced, ask the receptionist or administrative assistant before your interview. Also, make sure you know the gender of the person as well. Just the other day, I had an interview for a potential speaking engagement. The person interviewing me was named Morgan. I thought that, with a name like that, the person would be a woman. I was wrong! Other such names are Alex, Jaime, Joe, Pat and Tyler.

✓ Get directions

If you get lost and arrive late, you will give a poor first impression. The internet has many sites you can visit to get a map and directions on how to get to your interview. You can also call the company receptionist for directions. Make sure that you have the correct address.

Don't just go by what is in the phone book. Call to be sure. A friend of mine once went to the wrong location. The company moved, but it wasn't reflected in the latest phone book. Needless to say, he missed the interview and lost the job opportunity.

If you live close by, drive past the location a day or two before your interview. That way you will know for sure how to get there. Sometimes online driving instructions can vary quite a bit from site to site. It is always best to be safe rather than sorry.

✓ Pick out your interview clothes in advance

By planning ahead, you can concentrate solely on the interview and also avoid embarrassing mishaps. Years ago, I went to put on a suit the morning of an interview and I discovered my trouser zip was broken. I had to get a safety pin from the front desk of the hotel to keep my fly shut. Needless to say, I was so worried about my fly busting open, that the interview was a fiasco. Now I check my clothes at least a day or two before any important event.

You do not want to panic on the day of your interview because your favourite interview suit is at the cleaners, is dirty or has a button missing. Hang your clothes on a doorknob at least a day or two before any interview so that if something is wrong you have enough time to rectify the situation.

✓ Plan to arrive early

Arrange your schedule so you can show up for the interview at least 15 minutes early. That way you allow yourself some leeway for possible traffic delays. If you arrive really early, find a local coffee shop and relax for a few minutes. You can never look bad by being a few minutes early.

Being late to an interview, however, will destroy your chances of success. If you plan on being late, then you might as well chew garlic before the interview, too. I don't care if you get stuck on a train and neither will your interviewer. Being early gives you the chance to either get extra face time with interviewers or additional time to learn more about the company and its culture. Show up a little early and create that positive first impression.

Checklist Summary

✓ Any person you talk to throughout your job search may hold the keys to your next opportunity
✓ There are eight traits of ideal candidates
✓ Research your prospective companies and industries
✓ Create a list of possible interview questions
✓ Write down answers to those questions
✓ Practise, practise, practise
✓ Always go through a final interview checklist.

'Interviewers know within the first few seconds if they are interested in you. Be prepared!'

Secret No. 9
Interview to Win

■ The five rules of succeful interviewing.

Welcome to the interview, one of the most exciting aspects of the entire job search! This is the part of the job-hunting process that separates the winners from the losers. In this chapter, I am going to share with you the five rules of successful interviewing. Follow these rules and you will interview to win!

1. Visualise Success

Back in Secret No. 1, we talked about something so important that it needs repeating. In order to be successful, you have to visualise success. Before each interview, close your eyes and visualise the outcome you want. If you are having a phone interview, imagine the interviewer saying to you 'You are just the type of candidate we are looking for. I am going to recommend you for a second interview.'

If you are in a final personal interview, picture the interviewer standing up from the desk with a big smile and gleaming eyes, shaking your hand and saying 'You are exactly the type of person I am looking for, I would like to make you an offer. Congratulations!' Wow! Now that's powerful. Usually people imagine the worst happening when they go on an interview. Then they wonder why their expectations came true. You are a winner. Visualise success and you will achieve it!

Go for the win

In sports you may have heard someone describe a losing team as having 'played not to lose' rather than playing to win. In interviewing, it's natural to have this tendency because of the anxiety involved. However, if you approach the interview playing not to lose rather than interviewing to win, you will lose.

Don't be timid; be confident. Take some risks. No interview is life or death. Just remember everything happens for a reason. Don't put too much pressure on yourself. Have fun and go for victory.

Make yourself stand out from the crowd

Imagine that you are talking to several strangers a day. Who will you remember? You will recall those who are unique and leave you with either a very positive or very negative impression. If you are stiff, boring and seem in pain, you will be shown the door, not the job. However, if you are confident, exciting and fun to be around, you will generate interest and enthusiasm. You will leave interviewers with a thirst for more.

Typically, interviewers will ask each candidate the same core questions. They will be looking for specific answers. If you do not answer the first couple of questions with what interviewers want to hear, the interview is over – you have lost.

Ask the magical question

Imagine playing darts. It is hard enough to hit a bullseye as it is. Now, imagine wearing a blindfold and trying to hit the bullseye. Yet, when it comes to interviewing, most people interview blindfolded. Some get lucky and hit a bullseye. However, most don't and get rejected.

If there's one thing you should remember from this book it should be to ask the one magical question, in every interview, that can allow you to take off your blindfold and see your target.

The magical question

> 'If you had your ideal candidate for this position,
> what kind of qualities and characteristics
> would that person have?'

That's the magical question. Certainly, there are many ways you can phrase this question. You could also ask 'Describe your ideal candidate.'

When interviewers answer this question or a variation of it, they will articulate exactly the core strengths and competencies that they are looking for in their ideal candidates. Knowing this, you can tailor your answers throughout the rest of the interview. Focus on those strengths and competencies that demonstrate why you are indeed the right candidate for the position.

The key is for you to exemplify the traits and the qualities of the interviewer's ideal candidate. Why do you think politicians conduct so many polls? They do this to try to understand what the voting public wants from candidates. By asking the interviewers, early in the interview, to describe their ideal candidate, you will know what is important and what to focus on. Armed with this information, you will interview to win.

2. Maintain A Positive Attitude

No matter what I say in this chapter, if you do not feel good about yourself going into the interview, all your preparation will be for naught. If necessary, read Secret No. 1 again and remember that you are a great person. Whatever the outcome is, every interview offers an opportunity to learn. Each interview in which you participate gets you that much closer to the job you are supposed to have.

Believe in yourself

If you don't believe in yourself, neither will your interviewer. A positive attitude is contagious and interviewers thrive on it. Show confidence and enthusiasm.

Imagine for a moment that you're interviewing estate agents to sell your home. One agent comes in and fumbles through a predetermined presentation. He meekly gloats to you about how his company is No. 1 in your neighbourhood. He doesn't ask you what is important to you in your decision. He just assumes, because his agency is No. 1, that you should go with him.

Next, you interview a woman who walks in and says 'Wow, what a beautiful place. We'll have no problem selling this house. Look at the bathroom, the kitchen – this place is in move-in condition. When would you like to list it?'

I don't know about you, but as an interviewer, I would much rather go with the woman who showed genuine excitement about the place and was confident that it would be no problem to sell it. By far, she had a much more positive attitude and that is likely to help her succeed.

Interviewing is like selling

The best way to sell something is to show confidence and excitement. Go in there and act as if the job is the best thing that could ever happen to you and that you are the best thing that could ever happen to the company that is interviewing you. Communicate the confidence that says that the best decision the interviewer could make is to hire you.

Make interviewers feel good about themselves, their companies and the opportunities offered. You want interviewers to leave the interview on a high. When they do so, it makes it very difficult for any other candidate to win their affection. For example:

> I just want to let you know how much I appreciate you taking your valuable time to meet me. This position sounds so exciting and your company is the leader in the industry. I know I could make a great contribution to your ongoing success.

Be assertive about yourself. After all, if you don't speak highly of yourself, nobody will. Believe you are great and that any company would be lucky to have you as a part of their team.

When you are interviewing, don't put interviewers on a pedestal. If you do, you will be nervous and apprehensive. You have as much choice in this process as they do. No one is telling you what to do. You are your own person. After all, an interviewer may want to hire you on the spot but you might not like the company and choose not to accept their offer.

The most successful business relationships are those based on mutual trust, respect and equality. When you view yourself as an equal, you will perform at your peak, both in the interview and on the job.

Develop a personal mantra

Be confident, have fun and, most of all, be positive about the contribution you can make. Repeat to yourself that you are the best candidate out there. Refer back to the ideal job mission statement you created. Believe in your destiny and you will achieve it. The worst that can happens is that you are rejected. If your mission is your destiny, then one rejection will not stop you from achieving it.

Having a positive attitude will give you every chance to succeed in the interview and to have a wonderfully fulfilling life. Happiness in life is based not on the events that happen to you, but on how you choose to interpret those events. Look to the positive in every situation and you will achieve success and happiness beyond your wildest dreams.

3. Dress To Win

When you knock on the door, the first thing interviewers see is your appearance. Whether you are dating, job interviewing or meeting a stranger, first impressions are always important. More than 90% of all communication is non-verbal. You should try to look good. This definitely has a major impact on your chances of getting a job.

Seldom will the way you dress actually get you a job; but if you don't look good and dress professionally during the interview, you could easily lose one. Dress professionally.

Why is the way you dress so important? Think of flying. If you see the pilot wearing torn blue jeans and a stained white T-shirt, would you feel comfortable flying on that plane? Or would you rather fly with a pilot wearing a clean, smart, freshly pressed uniform? Interviewers would rather fly with the pilot wearing the uniform.

Your attire says a lot about you and how you feel about yourself. If you are clean-cut and professional looking, you will make a far greater first impression than if you look as though you've been dragged through a hedge backwards. Don't forget: people remember much more of what they see than what they hear. There's an old saying that goes 'a picture is worth a thousand words'. Need I say more? Dress professionally!

For men

Wear a professional and well-tailored suit
The best colours to choose are dark blue, grey, black or charcoal.
The suit should be plain or feature a subtle pinstripe pattern. Loud
pinstripes or bold plaids look great at dinners, but not at interviews.
The suit fabric should be mostly, if not 100%, wool. A small touch of
another material can help keep the suit's shape, but should be limited
to less than 25% of the total suit's composition.

Sport a high-quality and freshly pressed shirt
The shirt should always be bright white and nicely starched. You can
never go wrong with a white, long-sleeved shirt. If you want to wear
a blue shirt, save it for when you play poker, not interviewing. Short-
sleeved and coloured shirts are less formal and not appropriate in the
business setting. Save your short-sleeved shirt for the weekend.

Choose a tasteful tie and conservative shoes
The best styles for your tie are either traditional striped, geometric
or paisley. Red is perhaps the most conservative colour to choose and
yellow still makes for a great power colour. Make sure the tie you
choose is nicely pressed and free of any stains. You don't want the
interviewer spending half the interview wondering if that spot on your
tie is spaghetti sauce or soup.

   For your shoes, you can never go wrong with a traditional,
conservative style of shoe. Believe it or not, interviewers will look
at whether or not you have polished shoes. Polished shoes present a
professional image and demonstrate a good work ethic; so make sure
your shoes are polished and in good condition. If you wear shoes
with holes in the sole, or shoes that are scuffed up, you'll convey a
negative image.

Don't overlook your socks
I have seen men walk into interviews with cleanly pressed suit and
polished shoes, but mismatched socks. To avoid this problem, I suggest
keeping on hand a couple of pairs of new, plain-coloured socks that
are still in the package. That way, you know the colour and you know

for sure that they match. If you are not sure what colour to wear, black socks will go with almost any interview suit.

Make sure you are well groomed
Your hair should be stylish and short to medium in length. Unless you are interviewing for a creative position such as software development or musician, hair down to your shoulders is not a wise idea. If you have longer hair and do not wish to cut it, tie it back neatly to convey a professional image. Definitely make sure you are clean-shaven. If you have facial hair, keep it trimmed and shaped properly. Hands are also very important in conveying a positive and successful image. Your fingernails should be trimmed and clean or even manicured.

Minimise any jewellery
I recommend that you limit the jewellery on your hands to a wedding ring if you are married and nothing if you are not. Watches are also acceptable, as well as modest tie pins, tie clips and cuff links. Avoid wearing necklaces, lapel pins, chains, bracelets and religious jewellery. And whatever you do, do not wear an earring or a nose ring. If you want to work in a coffee shop, maybe you can get away with that. Otherwise, it just isn't appropriate business attire.

For women
Wear a professional and well-tailored suit
For more formal positions in industries such as banking, finance and accounting, wear a skirt suit or a fashionable trouser suit. For others, wearing trousers with a jacket or sweater top is perfectly acceptable. In selecting the colour, you need not limit yourself to plain grey, blue or black, but do not wear wild patterns.

Try to stay away from long jackets, as often they are just not flattering. If you are wearing a suit with a skirt, keep the skirt at a conservative length. Short skirts do not convey a professional image and can detract from your positive message. The key is to be tastefully stylish yet lean towards the conservative.

Depending on the style of suit you are wearing, you may want to wear either a blouse or a simple shirt. Either way, selection is very important. Your blouse or shirt should be plain in colour. If there is a print, it should be tasteful. The shirt or blouse should never be made of a transparent material. Items made of lace or satin should be avoided.

Match your outfit with fashionable shoes and tights

Wear shoes that are in 'like new' condition and complement your outfit. Heels should be totally intact. When it comes to tights, wear a conservative colour or a colour that complements the suit. Conservative choices are sheer, tan, taupe and black. If you wear bright-coloured or white stockings or tights, it can be distracting to interviewers and take away from your overall professional image.

Sport accessories that are tasteful, not distracting

In selecting a handbag or briefcase, choose one that complements your attire, either small or medium sized and made of leather. Large bags can be unsightly and create an appearance of disorganisation. Ideally, choose either a handbag or a briefcase, but not both. If you walk in with too much on your shoulders or in your hands, it can become awkward.

Hair, make-up and hands also leave an impression

Hair is a very important component in your overall presentation. Your hair should be manageable and preferably no longer than shoulder length. If your hair is long, you should wear it up or in a manner that is perceived to be stylish and professional. You don't want to look as if you just walked out of a beach house or a nightclub.

Make-up should be subtle and tasteful. Don't use too much: a bit of blusher and lipstick can be worn to accentuate your features. Depending on your complexion, natural colours such as browns or tans may be best. For your lips, soft reds, corals and pinks are the best colours. Use your best judgement. Too much make-up can be a detriment and a distraction.

Your hands should be well manicured. Fingernails should be painted either a conservative red, light pink, French style or with a clear polish. As an interviewer, for some reason, nothing would distract me more than a woman who had fingernails that were either different lengths, strange colours or improperly manicured.

In fact, when I interviewed musicians for my wedding reception, I rejected one band strictly because the lead singer's nail polish was peeling off. I didn't want that kind of an image at my wedding. I wanted a band that was professional and cared about their appearance. Your interviewers will too.

Keep jewellery to a minimum
If you are engaged or married, feel free to wear your wedding and engagement rings. However, try to avoid wearing other rings. I have seen women in interviews wear a ring on every finger. This just does not convey a professional image. In addition, it is very difficult for either party to give a good handshake, when someone is wearing too many rings. In shaking a person's hand, a firm grip is essential. Too much jewellery can inhibit that.

Earrings also have a bearing on your overall appearance. Too many earrings and extremely large earrings draw attention away from your presentation and message. Finally, do not wear religious jewellery. There is no need to bring religion into the interview. You want interviewers to focus on your skills and talent, not your faith.

Dress for success – not to make a fashion statement. Look professional, like an executive, not a nightclub patron. Dressing well is essential in creating a successful first impression.

For both men and women
Politicians provide great fashion guidance
Whether you are a man or a woman, one of the best indicators of what to wear on an interview is take note of what the politicians of your gender are wearing in their current public appearances and who is in office at the time of your interview. In the United States, often when a Republican is President, business attire becomes more conservative, in contrast to when the Democrats hold power. When in doubt, always err towards the conservative.

Freshen your breath

Believe it or not, breath contributes to your overall first impression. If your breath smells of garlic, onions, cigarettes or even coffee, you might offend interviewers.

Think about it: Do you feel comfortable when you are talking to a person with bad breath? Before the interview, brush your teeth, gargle with mouthwash and use a long-lasting breath freshener.

Clean your car

What kind of car are you driving? Do you have a clean car? If not, clean it before the interview. Interviewers may want to walk you to your car. You want to leave them with a positive impression, not a negative one. Is your car presentable? Or does it have more dents than a beer can that fell off a five-storey building? If your car is not presentable, hire one or take public transport.

Insider Tip

When I interviewed candidates, some would say how organised and polished they were. To see if they were telling me the truth or not, I would walk them out to their car. If their car had leftover fries from lunch or other loose articles strewn throughout, I would reject the person strictly on that basis alone. Why? Their actions didn't match their words.

Press your suit and use professional writing instruments

What kind of condition are your interview clothes in? Have you recently pressed your suit? If not, get it pressed. I can't think of a single article of business attire that looks better wrinkled than pressed. Wrinkles look sweet on bulldogs, not on interview candidates.

What about your notepad? Don't walk into the interview with a tatty yellow notepad. Get a professional one. Also, use a nice pen. Cross and Parker manufacture attractive and relatively inexpensive pens that present a very professional image. Don't walk into the interview with a cheap disposable pen. You will leave a bad impression.

Leave your mobile phones and pagers in the car
If you must keep your mobile phone or pager with you, turn it off before you go into the interview. Nothing is more annoying and disrupting than a mobile phone or beeper ringing during the interview. It is distracting, ruins the flow, and if you (GASP!) take the call, you convey the impression that your call is more important than your interview.

You can always return your calls later. That's what caller ID and voicemail are for. If your interview is not as important as an impending phone call or page, then probably you are interviewing for the wrong job. Give your interviewer the appropriate respect and turn off your phone.

4. Master The Three Phases Of A Winning Job Interview

To succeed in any interview, you must master each of the three phases of a winning job interview. Forget one phase and you can forget your chances of getting hired. Every moment of every interview can make or break your chances. You want to be as prepared and refined as possible, so you leave the interview with the job instead of the interviewer's foot on your behind.

1. Introduction

The first step to winning any job interview is your introduction. This is where that important first impression is made. It is during the introduction that interviewers see how you are dressed, how you shake their hand, and the presence you command when you enter a room.

You want to create a positive and lasting first impression. To do so, plan in advance how you are going to introduce yourself so you come across as confident, articulate, genuine and amiable. Write down a script and practise it over and over again. Smile, even as you practise.

Example:

Good morning, my name is _____ _____, currently of _____ company. I greatly appreciate you giving me the opportunity of meeting you today.

When greeting your interviewer, give a good, firm handshake
The handshake is usually one of the first and most telling events in
an interview. A firm, solid handshake demonstrates confidence and
enthusiasm and starts the interview in a positive fashion. However,
a wimpish handshake is quite the opposite. A good handshake shows
confidence and respect. A sweaty, weak and flimsy handshake says that
you lack self-esteem and you don't think you're the right person for
the job.

The key to the handshake is to be firm but not to squeeze. Be
assertive and show the interviewer that you think you are the right
person for the job.

Insider Tip

If your hands are clammy or sweaty, you can do something
to help. Right before the interview, wash your hands in warm
water and use lots of soap. Dry them off completely. The soap
will dry out your hands and help eliminate the sweat..

After the handshake, the interviewer will probably ask you to sit down.
At this time, if you see that the interviewer doesn't have a copy of
your CV on his or her desk, it is a good idea to take out an extra copy
and hand it to the interviewer

Example:

I have brought an extra copy of my CV for your convenience.

Also, if you have a business card, feel free to exchange it with
the interviewer at this time.

By having a strong introduction, interviewers will remember you.
The introduction step is usually the briefest step of the interview
process. However, it is one of the most important steps because first
impressions are always the most vivid and lasting. The interviewer will
probably be meeting several people, so you want to stand out and be
remembered positively.

As you are practising and preparing for your introduction, think about people in your life who have given you the best initial impressions. What was their aura? How did they look? What kind of expression did they have on their faces? Try to practise and replicate those features that provided the most positive and lasting first impressions.

Try to establish a good rapport right from the beginning
Developing good rapport is critical to any successful interview. Interviewers tend to like candidates who remind them of themselves. Think of the friends you have chosen to associate with throughout your life. Haven't most of those friends had qualities, characteristics and interests similar to yours? In establishing a positive rapport with interviewers, you want them, both consciously and subconsciously, to feel comfortable with you (almost like a friend) and believe that you have many things in common. This is done both verbally and non-verbally.

Verbal communication is essential in building a solid rapport
Interviewers each have their own unique styles of verbal communication. Tone of voice, pitch, rate and volume can all vary from one person to another. Voice can show a person's emotions and personality. Some may come across as pleasant and friendly, while others may be very serious and cold. You do not want to mimic interviewers, but you do want to speak in a similar manner.

For instance, say the interviewer has a very friendly tone and is extremely cheerful. Do not try to be overwhelmingly businesslike and monotone. You will fail miserably. On the other hand, if the interviewer is intensely businesslike and shows little emotion, your dialogue should respect that style.

If you try to be overly cheerful to a person who is not as light-hearted in nature, you won't succeed. It is also very important to notice the pitch, rate and volume of voice. If some interviewers speak in a low pitch, very slowly and softly, and you talk in a rapid, loud manner, you will overwhelm them.

Use words that are similar in conversation to those of the interviewer. If the interviewer uses emotional words such as feel, love and beautiful, then incorporate some of those words into your own conversation. Conversely, if the interviewer uses more factual-based words in conversation such as created, developed and structured, then you should use phrases that are similar.

People enjoy working with individuals who make them feel comfortable and who are like themselves. Use verbal communication to your advantage by talking in a fashion that matches that of your interviewers. If interviewers see some of their qualities in you, they will be much more receptive to what you have to say.

Non-verbal communication can be even more important
Ninety per cent, or more, of all face-to-face communication is non-verbal. Non-verbal communication includes appearance, facial expressions, posture, eye contact, gestures and scent. You can interpret non-verbal gestures to understand the true feelings of interviewers and use non-verbal communication to build positive rapport and to make a point.

Facial expressions can tell a lot about how well you are performing. If the interviewer is smiling and nodding in agreement to your message, keep going, you are doing fine. If you see a blank facial expression almost as if the interviewer is nodding off, then something is wrong. In this case, let the interviewer do more of the talking. Make your answers shorter and ask more questions.

If the interviewer has a very serious face, you should be serious too, otherwise you will agitate the interviewer. On the other hand, if the interviewer positively beams, then smile and be friendly.

Posture is also very important. If the interviewer is sitting in an open position and slightly reclined, this demonstrates a certain level of comfort or a general agreement with what you are saying. As such, you should also sit openly and slightly reclined. However, do not mimic. Instead, be discreet.

If the interviewer is sitting up straight and forward, do not sit in the chair like an oversized ball of putty. Position yourself like the interviewer. Otherwise, you will convey the impression that you could not care less how the interview turns out.

If the interviewer is sitting with arms crossed and straight as an arrow, then you are probably not doing too well. However, if the interviewer leans forward with the classic hand-on-the-chin pose then you may really have hit a hot button. Continue emphasising whatever you said that interested the interviewer.

What should you do when interviewers have their arms crossed?
Either you need to change what you are saying or you need to do something to get that person to relax. Typically, when interviewers stay with their arms crossed, they are either getting bored with what you are saying or for some reason they are not believing you. Ask if you are focusing on the information that the interviewer wants to discuss. Try to get the interviewer to talk more and get more involved.

Insider Tip

A trick I learned years ago, when interviewers' arms are crossed, is that you also should sit with your arms crossed. Then, slowly drop one arm and then the other. Often, interviewers will follow you and drop their arms as well. If not, then you are in trouble and you need to understand where you are going wrong.

If the interviewer asks you a vague question where you could easily ramble on, try to pinpoint the question. Say something like 'There is so much great information I could tell you, what would you like me to focus on first?'

When asked the famous 'tell me about yourself' question or asked your job history, try getting the question more focused. Ask something like 'Where would you like me to start?'

Eye contact is perhaps the most telling non-verbal clue. If an interviewer looks you straight in the eye, while listening to you, then you are communicating. If the interviewer is looking at the stuffed fish on the wall or the bubbles in the water cooler, then they are not hearing a word you are saying. Establish good eye contact with the interviewer. Eye contact shows that you mean what you say.

Gestures are also important and punctuate what you are saying. By smiling when you say something positive about yourself, or by being serious when you mention your work experience, you can emphasise your point. You can also lean forward or raise your hand to emphasise a particular strength or area of importance. Depending on the interviewer, gesture can make a positive or negative impact. If the interviewer is reserved and does not talk with his or her hands, you should follow suit.

Scent can also impact on your performance. Wear just enough perfume to create a light scent. Do not bathe in the bottle, as it can be offensive. Some people have perfume allergies and you don't want interviewers to have an allergic reaction to you. Be subtle in your scent, or forgo it completely.

However, don't forget to wear anti-perspirant or deodorant. If you smell like the inside of a gym locker, you will turn people off. If you have a tendency to sweat, wear light clothes and a jacket or blazer that will cover up your stains.

Make that first impression count
Subtly employ and embrace the verbal and non-verbal communication styles of the interviewer. The more similar you appear to the conscious and subconscious mind of the interviewer, the greater the chance you will have of succeeding in the interview.

Not only is non-verbal communication significant in understanding the interviewer and building rapport, it is critical in emphasising the message you're trying to get across. To enhance your non-verbal communication skills, look for non-verbal communication in your everyday life and practise it. Whether you are talking to a friend or meeting a business associate, consciously look for non-verbal clues. The more you practise, the better you will be able to use non-verbal communication and gestures in your interview.

To ensure a winning interview generate interest quickly
Communicate what you can do for the company and person interviewing you. At the beginning of your interviews, it's what you can do for them, not what they can do for you. Express enthusiasm and excitement. Use a golden nugget of information that will stimulate the interviewer.

In preparing for the interview, hopefully you identified key opportunities and contributions you could make to the success of the organisation. Revisit these items and develop a couple of simple sentences that convey an interesting fact about you that could intrigue the interviewer.

Example:

> I am excited about this opportunity. In my current position I have successfully reduced expenses by more than 35% and increased productivity by more than 20%. This is a great opportunity to leverage my experience and become an immediate asset to your company.

Another great way to generate interest is to ask the interviewer a variation of the magical question we discussed in the last chapter.

Example:

> If you had your ideal candidate for this position, what qualities and characteristics would be important to you?

The interviewer might mention characteristics such as motivated, team player, good communications skills and willingness to learn. Now you know what to emphasise. Focus on a couple of hot buttons.

Example:

> That's great. Throughout my career, I have consistently demonstrated that I am a very motivated person and I have always prided myself on being a part of the team.

Immediately, you can generate interest. If you don't ask interviewers what is important, you may end up talking about attributes that they don't care about. So make sure you ask the magical question at some point early on in your interview.

2. Qualification

The next phase of the interview is where both you and the interviewers see if there is a mutual fit. Remember all those questions you prepared for and answered earlier in this book? Now is the time you will put all that hard work to use.

In this phase, both you and the interviewers ask questions to qualify each other. If in the introduction you were not able to ask the question, 'If you had your ideal candidate for this position, what qualities and characteristics would that person have?' then you must work out a way at the beginning of this phase to ask it.

Examples of qualifying questions

- What is it about your company that you enjoy the most?
- What are the biggest challenges that you are facing today?
- What traits do your top performers have in common?
- What are the key attributes that make your company better than others in the industry?
- How do you reward top performers?
- If I exceed expectations, what is the typical timeframe to get reviewed?
- Do you have any additional questions?
- What is the next step in this interview process?
- When do you expect to make a decision on this position?
- How quickly could I start, if I was accepted for this position?

Ask positive and assumptive questions – ones that foster feedback and communication. These kinds of questions will impress the person interviewing you. By asking questions such as these, you display a confidence that says 'I know I am the right person for this job. Why look further?'

Don't be afraid to ask questions. You have the right to know the answers. Otherwise, how will you know if the position interests you and if it is the right job for you? Interviewers will sense your confidence and will be more than happy to answer your questions.

Ask questions at the appropriate time
Don't just fire one question after another at interviewers, especially
at the beginning. Usually interviewers will ask you at the end of this
phase if you have any questions. That is the best time to ask them.
Also, whatever you do, don't ask about sick leave or holiday allowances
during your interview. If you get an offer, then you can ask HR about
that. It just isn't relevant to ask those types of questions early in the
interviewing process. If you do, you'll come across as work-shy!

Insider Tip

Interviewers are schooled on making you do most of the
talking. However, one of the best ways to succeed in an
interview is to get the interviewer to do more of the talking
instead. In sales, we have a saying 'We were given two ears
and one mouth for a reason: we should listen twice as much
as we talk.' The same holds true for you.

The qualification phase is when interviewers justify or refute their
first impressions. In most cases, interviewers try to justify their initial
feelings. If they had a great feeling about you from the beginning, they
will look for answers to their questions that confirm those feelings.

Again, throughout this phase as well as the entire interview, the
more you can tailor your conscious and subconscious messages
towards the interviewer's concept of an ideal candidate, the better your
chances of success.

Review your strengths
Towards the end of the qualification phase, make sure you summarise
your strongest points. Restate what interviewers say they are looking
for in their ideal candidates. Make sure you know exactly the type of
individual they want, otherwise you could still lose in the final phase
of the interview.

Be sure to ask at some point if there is any additional information
that the interviewer would like to discuss. Ask 'Are there any other

questions that you have for me at this time?' Then, position yourself for a powerful close.

3. Summary/close

This is the best part of the interview. This phase is very similar to closing arguments in a court case. It is here that you make your final impression. Just as a lawyer wants to leave the jury with a final statement that is strong and persuasive, so do you. After all, the second most important impression after your first impression is your final one. So, make it good!

By this point in the interview, you should have a good idea whether or not you have a chance of getting the job. This is where you go for the close – a job offer. In going for the close, be confident and excited. Summarise your skills and relate how your expertise will benefit the interviewer and the company.

Example of a strong closing statement:

> I want to thank you for giving me the opportunity to meet you. This job sounds exciting and I know I can make an immediate impact. You mentioned that reducing costs and improving efficiencies are two of your most important objectives. Having reduced expenses by more than 15% in my last position and by increasing productivity by 20%, I am confident that I can jump in and immediately contribute to the ongoing success of your team. I am looking forward to the opportunity. Once again, I greatly appreciate your time and efforts on my behalf.

When interviewers want to hire you, they often will become as excited as you will. They'll show enthusiasm and give specific timeframes as to when they will follow up. If they don't, you have a problem. It is not a positive sign when interviewers are inconclusive or vague at the end of an interview. Typically, when interviewers are evasive at the end, it means they have some sort of objection or reservation about you.

Try to pin them down. Ask 'What is the next step in the decision-making process?' If, after asking that question, the interviewer is still elusive, you could be really bold and ask a pointed question that will definitely elicit a response, such as 'Is there anything that would prevent you from wanting to employ me?' When you ask a question that is bold and pointed like that, it gives you an opportunity to identify the objection or objections that the interviewer has about you. I recommend asking a question like that only if you think that for some reason the interview is not ending on a good note and there is something wrong that needs to be brought out.

Either way, during the close of the interview, maintain your composure, and remain positive, self-assured and enthusiastic. As we have discussed before, if you do not exemplify these traits, you will be shown the door, not the job. Give interviewers a reason to want to hire you. Act like a winner, and interviewers will perceive you as one.

Insider Tip

Never ask an interviewer 'When will you get back to me?' Interviewers would rather gargle with razor blades than hear that question. It is much better to say 'What is the next step in the decision-making process?'

The close of the interview is also similar to the final seconds of a football match. Sometimes, if you have outscored your opponents throughout the interview, the close is just a formality. At other times, you may need to make that final shot to win the game. Before each interview, picture yourself making that game-winning shot and you will succeed. Practise that final shot over and over again.

5. Have Fun

The most important aspect of a successful interview is to have fun. The interview is one of the most exciting aspects of job hunting. Enjoy it and have fun with the whole process. You may be thinking, 'Interviewing gives me headaches and sweaty palms! How can it possibly be fun?' Interviewing is fun if you have the right approach and the right attitude.

Interviewing is nothing more than a game. There are winners and there are losers. In order for you to be the winner, you have to have better preparation, strategy, attitude and performance than your competitors.

When I interviewed people in the past, I thoroughly enjoyed many of the interviews. Individuals who were confident in themselves, and knew how to have fun, were always the most enjoyable to interview. By coincidence, those were typically the candidates I hired.

As an interviewer, I wanted to come out of the interview pumped up. I wanted to be excited about whom I was about to employ. Sometimes I was so enthusiastic, I couldn't wait to offer the person the job. When you generate that kind of enthusiasm, you win!

As in sports, talent alone doesn't win

Don't worry if you lack 'experience'. Often, the sports teams that recruit and possess the best players still don't win. Regardless of the sport, every year there seems to be at least one team that, at the beginning of the season, no one thought would win. On paper, they looked like just an average team. Yet somehow, they reach the playoffs and sometimes win the championship.

The reason they make it that far is that they put no pressure on themselves to win, they just expect it. They approach the game to win and have fun. Being more relaxed and confident, the end result is they end up winning. Have you ever noticed that the people who have the most fun on their jobs tend to be the most successful people in their profession? Interviewing is the same. Have fun!

Treat interviewing like the game that it is

Why not see how many offers you can get? Why not try to anticipate questions before they are asked? I used to have fun by trying to guess how the people would look, just by thinking about their name. With the attitude that interviewing is like a game, you will be much more relaxed and confident.

Laugh at your learning experiences. The more fun you have, the better you will perform. After all, interviewing is a game for interviewers as well. They may have fun by seeing how you handle a tough question or how you stack up against the others. Some interviewers ask crazy questions just to make candidates squirm.

One of my friends, a fellow sales manager at a company I worked for, asked interviewees 'Why are manhole covers round?'

In asking this question, he looked for how candidates handled a completely unrelated and utterly pointless question. He also looked to see how someone handled a situation where they did not know the answer. After all, one of the last things managers want is for an employee to lie or make up an answer. He rejected many candidates because they stumbled and tried to make up an answer. It's better for you to admit you don't know the answer and ask if you can follow up with the answer at a later time.

If someone makes up an answer to this question in the interview, what would they do on the job in front of a customer? Managers never want their people saying something to the customer of which they are not sure. Instead, good employees will tell the customer they will research the answer and get back to them.

If you are ever asked a question where you do not know the answer, be honest and say you don't know. Say that you would be more than happy to research the answer and get back to them. Lying and making up answers to questions is the surest way to be rejected.

In fact, if you are nervous and not sure about a tough question, try to make light of the situation. Say something like 'Well, that's an interesting question! I have to admit you've stumped me. Let me think about that one for a second.' Or you could say, 'Hmm, that is one of the best questions an interviewer has ever asked me. May I ask how you would answer that question?'

When you add some levity to the situation, it helps to loosen you up and provides valuable stalling time for you to contemplate your answer.

Why manhole covers are round

The answer is that a circular-shaped lid, unlike a square or an oval, won't fall through the opening. There's no way to position a round cover to slip through a slightly smaller hole of the same shape. That's because a circle has a constant width (the same width all the way around).

However, an oval has a shape that is longer than it is wide. Thus, you can always find a way to slip an oval lid through a hole of the same shape. That's also true of a square or a six-sided, hexagonal cover. If you try to cut those shapes out of a piece of paper, you will see that you can slip the cut-out piece right through the opening created by the cut-out.

Insider Tip

As an interviewer, there was one question I always asked candidates to make the interview more fun:
'Why should I hire you instead of one of the other candidates I have interviewed?'
I couldn't wait to ask that question. It was amazing how differently people answered it. How will you answer that question when it comes up in your next interview?

There are many ways to have fun with interviewing

You can win if you relax and do not put pressure on yourself. Look at every interview as an opportunity for you to sell yourself, an opportunity to learn, and an opportunity to have fun. Remember, if you get the hook around the neck, so what? You will have gained knowledge from the experience and you will be that much closer to your dream job.

Try rewarding yourself

To add fun to the process, a friend of mine would treat herself to something nice after each interview – regardless of how it went. That way she always looked forward to the interview. Maybe you want to reward yourself with a nice lunch or a relaxing massage. Whether you choose to reward yourself after each interview or to treat each interview like a game, you can have fun with the entire process.

You have a say too

Yes, you have to sell yourself. However, don't be afraid to make the company sell itself to you. You have a lot of talent and positive qualities. Good employees are not easy to find. There are a lot of mediocre people out there. Don't sell yourself short. You have a tremendous amount to offer and you should be proud of yourself. If interviewers cannot express why you should work for their company, then maybe that company is not worth joining.

Each interview is an opportunity to shine, an opportunity to learn, and an opportunity to get your ideal job. Visualise success, believe in yourself and your ability to succeed, dress to win, master the three phases of a winning interview – and have fun.

Do so and you will win!

Checklist Summary
- ✓ Visualise success
- ✓ Maintain a positive mental attitude
- ✓ Remember: you are the interviewers' equal
- ✓ Dress to win
- ✓ Master the three phases of a winning job interview
- ✓ Non-verbal communication is often more important than verbal
- ✓ Treat interviewing as a game and have fun!

'Before each interview, close your eyes and visualise the outcome you want.'

Secret No. 10

Follow Up and Close the Deal

- Summarise the interview
- Three components of a winning thank-you note
- Accept good offers with enthusiasm
- Reject bad offers with dignity
- Negotiate debatable offers with confidence.

Phew! The interview is over – or is it? Many people make the fatal mistake of assuming the interview process is over once they walk out of the door. That couldn't be further from the truth. Just because your face-to-face time is over, it doesn't mean you should sit idly by the phone waiting for it to ring. There are many things you should do both immediately after the interview and in the hours and days to come.

Summarise The Interview

Immediately after each interview, drop into a nearby coffee shop, library or some other public place and sit down to write some notes that summarise the interview you have just had. If you have just completed a phone interview, then do so at your desk.

Make sure you have the correct spelling of the names of all the people you talked to. For personal interviews, hopefully you asked each person for a business card.

Write down key points you discussed with each person throughout each phase of the interview. This will help you prepare for future interviews with that company and also help you determine if you are interested in the position.

Often, I have been saved by the fact that I took notes after an interview. When talking with several companies, you'd be surprised how hard it is to remember what has been said. Also, in subsequent interviews, you may want to refer back to what was mentioned in an earlier interview.

Example:

> In speaking with your head of sales, I learned that your company
> is very service-oriented. How do you maintain this image?

By writing down notes immediately after the interview, the
information you have just received will remain fresh in your mind.
This information will also be helpful when you compare one position
with another. One company may have better working conditions
while another may have a position that is more stimulating. By
having good notes, you can accurately determine which job is best
for you.

Rate your performance

Also, when summarising the interview, rate your performance during
each phase of the interview. Summarise the areas where you think you
did well, and note the areas where you need to improve. This will help
you learn from each interviewing experience. Later, you can practise
on those areas that need improvement.

When you take the time to summarise each interview, suddenly,
there is no such thing as a bad interview. You can learn from the
experience. The only way you can fail on an interview is if you don't
take the time to learn from it.

Make Sure You Say Thank You

Within a few hours of your interview, you should type a thank-
you note to each person with whom you spoke. If you have good
handwriting, a handwritten note on good stationery can be an
excellent touch – even send the receptionist or secretary a thank you.
You might be surprised to discover how much power a receptionist
or secretary can have in an organisation. They can either help or
destroy your chances of getting your ideal job. Once you have typed
up your letters, either email them or send them via Special Delivery
or first-class post.

Why go to this time and expense? Well, if you really want the job,
then you need to do what it takes to get it. I can guarantee you that

if an interviewer is on the fence and not quite sure which person to choose, a simple thank you can make all the difference. If you send an email or next-day delivery letter, that person is going to say, 'Wow! That's the kind of person I want to hire!'

I remember a time when I was really torn between two candidates I interviewed for a district manager position on the West Coast. Both people did a great job interviewing. Both were polished and had excellent experience. I actually tried to convince the company to allow me to recruit both of them. Unfortunately, upper management said no. The first applicant I interviewed emailed me immediately upon her return to California, that same day. In the email, she told me how excited she was about the opportunity and how successful she would be in the position. The second candidate I interviewed took more than two days to thank me. Well, as you might imagine, I ended up hiring the first person because of the simple fact that she thanked me in a more timely and enthusiastic fashion.

When writing a thank-you note, there are three components you should include to make the message as powerful as possible. When you include these items as a part of your message, you will leave a positive and lasting impression.

The Three Components Of A Winning Thank-you Note

1. Thank interviewers for the opportunity

As simple as it sounds, start out your thank-you notes by thanking the interviewers for their time and consideration. Then, tell them how excited you are about the opportunity. Your interviewers' time is valuable. They appreciate it when you show some gratitude.

2. Summarise why you are the best candidate

Provide a brief summary of the qualities that the interviewer identified as important in an ideal candidate. Then, show why you are the best person for the job. After interviewing several candidates, the minds of recruiting managers can become as cluttered as a house after a birthday party. Reminding them why you are the best person for the job may just be the thing that puts you on top.

3. Go for the close

End your thank-you notes by once again thanking them and saying
that you very much hope you will have the opportunity to be part
of their winning team. Your thank-you notes should be short, to the
point, and convincing. You don't want to say too much – you might
'buy back the sale'. However, you want to say enough to remind
them why you are the best candidate for the position and that you want
the job!

Sample thank-you note

Dear Jamie,
Thank you for taking the time to meet me today to discuss the
technical support managerial position at High Tech Industries.

This is certainly an exciting opportunity, and I would very
much welcome the opportunity to be a part of your winning
team. During our discussion, you mentioned that your main goals
are to reduce employee turnover, improve customer satisfaction
and reduce the number of abandoned calls coming into technical
support. Having reduced employee turnover by more than 20%,
and significantly improved the overall customer experience
for my previous employer, I am confident that I can help you
achieve your goals and make an immediate contribution to your
organisation.

If there is any further information I can provide,
please feel free to contact me on +44 (0)123 456789 or
tbermont@10stepjobsearch.com. Once again, thank you for your
consideration.

Yours sincerely,

Todd Bermont

Do The Small Things That Make A Big Difference

In interviewing, as well as in life, it is sometimes the smallest things that can make the biggest difference. By doing the little things like saying thank you via email, you can make a difference. What's the worst that can happen? You waste a few minutes of your time. At least you will be at peace with yourself knowing you did everything you could to get the job.

One of the most frustrating things is failing at something because you didn't give it your best shot. So what if it takes a couple of extra hours or you spend a couple of additional pounds? In the grand scheme of things, what's the big deal?

If you had a great interview, you properly follow up, and if you pay attention to the small things that make a big difference, you may well get the job. Realistically, when interviewers like you, they will get back to you quickly, usually, within a couple of days. Unless otherwise specified, it should never take more than a week to hear back from an interviewer.

If you don't hear back from the interviewer in a timely fashion, don't hesitate to call. Time, energy, expense and emotions are invested in each of your interviews. You have a right to know where you stand. If more than a week goes by and you have not heard from the interviewer, then by all means call the interviewer.

If you get voicemail, then leave a professional message such as:

Good afternoon Jerry, this is Todd Bermont. I wanted to call to thank you for taking the time to interview me last week for the accounting position. It's an exciting opportunity and one that I know I can succeed in. I just wanted to follow up with you to say that I greatly enjoyed our conversation and to see where things stood. I look forward to hearing from you at your earliest convenience. I can be reached on 0123 456 789. Once again, thank you for your time.

Then, give it a few days. If you still don't hear back, then keep calling until you reach the interviewer. The chances are that if you don't hear back in a timely fashion you haven't got the job. But keep calling in any case. The only way you will truly learn from the experience is to understand why they didn't want to hire you.

If you didn't get the job, then ask them why. Ask a question like 'Jerry, I thought I was an ideal person for the job. Would you mind telling me where I fell short, so I can learn from the experience?'

The interviewer may bring out an objection you can handle. If that is the case, you might be able to turn around the situation. But, if not, at least you will know why you were rejected. Often, it is something you cannot control. Either way, it is good to know why.

By reading this book, you should have many more good interviews than bad. I know that you can interview to win. You will succeed and get many job offers. Keep the faith!

Give Each Offer Careful Consideration

So, if all goes well, you will get the job offer. Now what? For sure, the greatest prize of all in your job search is to get a job offer. But just because you have an offer doesn't mean your job search is over. You have to analyse the offer and decide if it is the right job for you. Then, you have to follow the appropriate steps to ensure a happy ending.

Contain your emotions

Regardless of the quality of the offer, contain your emotions. It is easy to get caught up in the heat of the moment. By remaining calm, you will make the right career decision. Choosing a job is one of the most important things you can do in life. Don't rush into a decision.

Ask yourself some important questions

Before making a decision, ask yourself a few questions about the opportunity. I have listed 10 questions that I have used in the past to evaluate job offers that I received:

1 Is this a position I really want?
2 Are they offering me enough money and benefits?
3 Is this a short-term position or one with a good career path?
4 Will my personality match well with this company?

5   In three years, will I still want to work for this company?

6   Do I want to work for this type of boss?

7   Is the position in alignment with my purpose, mission statement and values?

8   Is this a job I can be passionate about?

9   Is this a job I can succeed at, yet still have a balance in my life?

10 Can I truly picture myself in this position?

Make a decision and follow up

Once you have studied the offer, it's time for that moment of truth: to call the interviewer and either accept the offer, reject it or try to negotiate it. For the remainder of this chapter, I will give you some guidelines that will help you, regardless of your decision. Just to get to this point is fantastic. Whatever your decision may be, you should be very proud of yourself to have made it here. I know that I am proud of you for investing your valuable time and money in this book, and I am confident that you will have many opportunities to evaluate job offers in the very near future. Let's take a look at what you should do when these offers start flowing in.

Accept Good Offers With Enthusiasm

Call interviewers in a timely fashion. There is no reason to wait too long. Reply in a timeframe that is long enough to show that you are not desperate, but short enough to demonstrate your excitement at the job. I recommend thanking the person for the offer and saying that you will get back within a day or two with a final decision.

You want to convey an image that you are in demand. However, it is perfectly acceptable, if you are happy with the offer, to accept it immediately. Only you will be able to judge the situation and do what is right. Either way, thank them so much for the offer and show your excitement.

Limit your conversation

You do not want to 'buy back the sale'. Interviewees often make the mistake of talking too much and actually losing or 'buying back' the job offer. Don't make this mistake.

When you do decide to accept, do so in an excited tone. Accept the position and restate your enthusiasm. Then, ask what the next step should be, and when and where you should report to work. Most importantly, thank interviewers for offering you a job and give them the impression that they have made the right decision!

Example of accepting an offer:

> Hello Mr _____ this is _____ speaking. I want to thank you so much for the job offer and I am calling you to accept. [Be enthusiastic!] It'll be good to know in due course what the next step in the process could be. [Pause!] But again, thank you so much for giving me this opportunity. I look forward to talking again soon.

When you show up for your first day

The absolute final step in the job-hunting process is your first day of work. Give it your best. As with making that initial impression in your interview, when you start a new job, you only get one opportunity to give a first impression. Make it count.

Be on your best behaviour. Wear your nicest clothes. Nothing is official until you sign all the paperwork. As you did for the interview, show up early and be as enthusiastic as can be. Your goal for your first day should be to ensure that your new boss is thrilled to have made the decision to employ you.

Ideally, everyday thereafter you also want to give it your all. That is the best way to have a career full of joy and happiness. I for one know that when I have given my fullest efforts I always feel better at the end of the day. When you give 110% you'll feel joy and satisfaction as well.

Reject Bad Offers With Dignity

Make sure you are making the right decision

The job hunt can be a very emotional journey. Various emotions can cause you to make rash decisions. Before you decide to formally reject an offer, make sure the position fails to match your criteria of an ideal job. Review the 10 elements of job satisfaction on page 49.

The key is to take your emotions out of the decision and look at the situation objectively. If, after doing so, you are not comfortable with the job, then reject it. If you are not sure, ask some of your friends and family for advice. And don't hesitate to ask your interviewer any questions you are not sure of.

Respond quickly and courteously

If you want to reject the offer, give interviewers a chance to look elsewhere. Try your best to respond in a timely fashion. You never want to 'burn any bridges'. A phone call or a letter is appropriate. I personally prefer a phone call, but that is up to you.

Either way, thank the interviewers for their time. Flatter them a bit: say it has been a tough decision, but it is not the ideal fit at this time.

Try to keep your options open

Mention that you are very impressed with the company and that you would like to keep your options open if an opportunity with a better fit opens up in the future. You never know when in the future you might want to work for the company. Try to be as complimentary as possible towards the person and the company and part on gracious terms.

Example of how to reject an offer:

> Hello Ms _____, this is _____ speaking. I want to thank you so much for the job offer. Unfortunately, at this time I have to decline. I am extremely impressed with your company and this has been a very difficult decision. The offer just isn't the right fit for me at this time. I greatly appreciate the time you spent with me and I'd like to keep the dialogue open for the future. Again, thank you so much for your time.

Negotiate Debatable Offers With Confidence

What if you really like your potential employer and boss, yet you are disappointed in the offer they gave you? What should you do? This is really a touchy subject. First, review the questions from earlier sections of this chapter. Then, go over the exercise you did on determining your ideal job.

See how closely this offer matches the criteria of your ideal job. Look at all the accompanying perks. If you still feel the offer is short of your expectations, then be honest with yourself and try to negotiate for more. This is a difficult topic, because in any negotiation you can lose, and in this case of negotiating an offer, you can lose the job altogether.

However, if you are not going to be happy working for what they proposed, then you have no other alternative than to negotiate. The last thing you want to do is to accept a job with which you are not happy.

In what follows I will share with you seven steps to a successful job-offer negotiation. If you follow these, you have a solid chance of scoring more favourable terms and conditions.

1. Research The Market

Before entering into any job negotiation, research the market to see how your job offer compares with others. Look at the title of the position you are being offered. For instance, a director will typically get paid more than a manager. See what comparable titles earn in your targeted industry. In doing this research, you will have an idea of how your offer compares with others and you will have an indication of how much negotiating room you have.

2. Exhibit Confidence

When negotiating with interviewers, you need to maintain your confidence. Any weakness here will cause interviewers to stick to their original offer. They may even yank the offer off the table altogether. If you come across as confident, and willing to lose the job if necessary, you are more likely to get a better offer. After all, out of all the people they interviewed, the company chose you – this means they want you, so be confident!

However, being confident does not mean being demanding or cocky. People don't like to be told what they have to do. Show balance in your approach. Be firm, not demanding!

Example of how to show confidence:

> I really appreciate your offer and I know I will be a tremendous asset to your company. However, I must tell you that I was expecting a salary of about £5,000 more. The position is exciting and I'd very much welcome being part of the company, but unfortunately I cannot accept the job under these terms. Is there any way we can meet somewhere in between?

3. Create Demand

In any negotiation, when one party is in demand – or has more control of a situation – typically, the other party realises they need to be flexible. Remember our dating analogy from earlier in the book? Rightly or wrongly, many people feel that if their significant other is also seeing other people, they need to be more generous and considerate towards that person. In other words, couples are sometimes more flexible with each other when they are not exclusive.

Negotiating for a job is very similar. You want to show an image that other companies are interested in you and that your skills are in demand. Convey the message that there are additional offers or opportunities out there.

Example of how to create demand:

> I have been looking at several companies, and though I am the most excited about your position, I must say that the numbers you are offering don't quite match my expectations.

4. Demonstrate Excitement

It is critical to show excitement for the job at hand. If you do not appear enthusiastic about the job, then they will not sweeten your offer. On the other hand, if you are excited and confident and they are just a few dollars short, then you will have a better chance of getting an improved offer.

5. Find A Win-Win

For any negotiation to be successful the end result has to be a win-win situation. That means both sides have to feel like they are better off as a result of the negotiation. Many companies will purposely leave a little room for negotiation. The key here is to show how the company will benefit by giving you more money. You also need to demonstrate that you are willing to give as well.

Example of a win-win:

> As I mentioned earlier, the offer is about £10,000 short of my expectations. I feel sure that my contribution will more than make up for that difference, but, if we can meet somewhere in the middle, I can enthusiastically accept your position.

The key here is to start with a figure that is higher than what you are willing to settle for so that you can meet in the middle. For instance, if the offer was £2,000 less than you had hoped, then say it was £5,000 less and ask to meet in the middle. If the offer was £5,000 less, then say it was £7,000–£10,000 less than your expectations. The same technique can be used in regard to holiday time and other aspects of the offer. If the company wants you badly enough, they will be willing to negotiate. Just realise your limits and don't push for too much.

6. Expand The Playing Field

Another aspect of negotiating is to expand the scope of the negotiation. For instance, let's say the company offered you £5,000 less than your expectation. Would you accept the offer if they increased your allowances or if they granted you an extra week's holiday? Sometimes companies have more flexibility in one area than another, so be creative. Don't limit your negotiations to just salary.

If salary remains a key sticking point, but you really want the job, then try negotiating for a review (for a pay rise) after three or six months, instead of the standard one year. Some companies are willing to accept this idea because it lowers their risk. However, if you agree to this, ensure you get it in writing.

Many a manager has either moved on or conveniently forgotten items such as this. By having the outcomes of your negotiations in writing, there is no room for interpretation.

7. Once Again, Go For The Close

After you have set out on the table what you want, whether it is a higher salary or more benefits, finish your negotiations by once again going for the close. Summarise your excitement about the position and exhibit confidence that you can become an immediate asset to the company.

Example of going for the close:

> I cannot tell you how excited I am about this position, and feel sure I can make an immediate contribution to your team. I look forward to hearing back from you on this request. Once again, thank you for your time and consideration.

There are many ways to come to a resolution that makes both sides happy. Decide what you are willing to accept, and go for it. Just be aware that the company always reserves the right to refuse negotiation and may tell you to take it or leave it.

If their final offer is still unacceptable, then reject it. After all, you want to be happy. Just do so with compassion and dignity. Let's face it, remuneration is an important factor in job satisfaction. It cannot be ignored if you want a position you can enjoy and stick with for any length of time. If a company is not willing to negotiate, then it is not a very flexible organisation and probably not one you want to work for anyway.

Only you will be able to decide what is right. Negotiation can bring you a better offer but it can also cause you to lose your offer. Weigh all the risks and potential rewards before you enter into any negotiating process. Then approach the negotiation with confidence. Visualise the outcome you want, and go for it!

For more tips and techniques on how to negotiate your job offers, once again, go to your favourite search engine on the Web. Type in search phrases such as 'negotiating job offers', 'salary negotiation' and 'free job search negotiation tips'. You'll find many sites that can give you excellent advice.

Checklist Summary

✓ After each interview, summarise what you discussed and learned.
✓ Assess your performance.
✓ Identify areas of improvement.
✓ Send a thank-you note as quickly as possible.
✓ If you get rejected, ask why.
✓ Respond to offers in a timely fashion.
✓ Accept good offers with enthusiasm.
✓ Reject bad offers with dignity.
✓ Negotiate debatable offers with confidence.

'Visualise the outcome you want and go for it!'

Some Final Thoughts

Congratulations! You have now the foundation you need to be successful in your job search. You have learned everything from developing a positive attitude to selling yourself in the interview to following up, closing the deal and getting the offer.

I hope this has been a fun and rewarding experience for you. I know I have enjoyed sharing my knowledge and time with you. These secrets, tips and techniques will undoubtedly help you achieve success.

Before we can conclude, though, there is one secret that I have yet to mention. Unfortunately, without this secret, you cannot succeed in your job hunt. On the other hand, if you embrace this secret, you'll be well on your way to getting the job you want at a salary you desire.

Secret No. 11: Take Immediate Action

You must take the knowledge you have gained from this book and take immediate action. I cannot tell you how many people I have met who have just sat on their laurels waiting for a job to drop in their lap. Then they wonder why they can't find a job.

I know the concept of taking action is not easy. Change is always scary. But without action, you cannot succeed. Sometimes it is easier to start by taking baby steps. What I have found helpful is to put together a daily to-do list. I include items such as 'research 10 companies' and 'make five phone calls'. When you write out a step-by-step list of what you have to do, it makes things much easier.

Jump in ... the water's fine

I am sure you have been in a swimming pool or hot tub before. Have you ever stepped in and felt the pool was too cold or the tub too hot? I know I have. Every time I went into a pool or tub one foot at a time, it was always difficult. I discovered that it was much easier just to jump in. The first couple of seconds are always tough, but the body adjusts quickly. Beginning your job search is the same as jumping into a pool.

If you start too slowly, or not at all, you will never fully get into it and you will prolong your misery. But if you jump into the job hunt with both feet you will realise it is not so bad. Just jump in and you'll do fine.

Like a locomotive, it takes time to pick up speed

But once you build up the momentum, you cannot help but succeed. The faster you start, the more momentum you will pick up. The more momentum you pick up, the greater your chances will be of getting the job you have always wanted.

Now it's up to you

Hopefully, by now you have completed the exercises in this book and you are ready to begin your job search. If not, complete the exercises as soon as possible and start implementing the secrets. Having read this book, you now have the foundation necessary to succeed.

If you are employed, you can either stay in a job you are not happy with or you can take action and live out your dreams.

If you are unemployed, you can either stay unemployed or you can go out there and start selling yourself.

If you are a student, you can either remain a permanent student and not deal with reality, or you can get excited, jump in and get your dream job.

I cannot make the ultimate decision for you. Only you can!

You Are Great!

I know you are a fantastic person with fantastic credentials. You are the type of person that any company would be fortunate to have on their pay roll. It is my sincere hope and desire that you go out there and get the job you really want.

My purpose in writing this book is simple. I want to help as many people as possible improve their lives, by getting the jobs they want, quickly and easily. If I have helped motivate you to find the job you want, then I have only partially achieved my objectives. My ultimate goal is for you to go out there and actually get that job of your dreams.

Go out there and do it!

Jump in and, most importantly, have fun! Life is too short to get stressed over the job search. If you follow what is discussed in this book, you will succeed. Relax, take action, and be proud of who you are. I am proud of you for having the courage and taking the time to read this book.

Are you smiling and having fun yet? If not, you should be. By following the advice given in this book, you will succeed!

You Will Get The Job You Really Want

You are among the select few who can conquer any challenge presented to you in an interview. The fact that you have taken the time to read this book and improve your skills demonstrates that you are a winner. By spending the time you have just invested in yourself, you will get that job you really want. Also, hang on to this book for future reference. Keep it with you in your car. The job search is nothing more than a game. Be prepared and confident. If you want to stay in touch or provide any feedback, please feel free to visit my website on the internet at www.10stepjobsearch.com.

Believe that you are no. 1 and have fun!

At this time, I would like to thank you again for investing your hard-earned time and money in this book. I wish you every success in your job hunting as well as in your personal life. It has been a tremendous honour to be able to share these moments with you. Once again, thank you! Now go out there and get that job of your dreams!

Best wishes to you!

Frequently Asked Questions

Since publishing my first book, I have had the privilege of coaching several clients, speaking in front of many groups and appearing as a guest on numerous radio and television programmes – including CNN and FOX. As a result, I have had the opportunity to talk with thousands of job seekers just like you.

Interestingly, there have been 10 common questions about the job-search process. I thought I would share these with you to give you that final edge you need to get that job you really want.

1. When Are the Best Times To Interview?

Most companies will interview more than one person for a given position. As with a horse race or motor race, your 'post' or 'pole' position for the interview can often influence your chances of success.

How does timing affect your opportunity? If you are the fifth person to interview, and the third person made an incredible impression, you'll have a difficult hurdle to overcome. The precedent will have been set and the interviewer may have already made up his or her mind.

You should always try to be the first person to interview. By being first, you can set the expectation level. Everyone will have to measure up to you. Also, as with first impressions, the interviewer will remember the most about the person who interviewed first. If you have an outstanding interview, it will be tough for anyone after you to succeed.

Tuesdays and Thursdays are the optimal days to interview

Mondays are bad days because they are often spent getting organised and planning for the week. Wednesdays are sometimes unpleasant because people like to take a midweek break, and it is a typical day for internal meetings. Fridays are poor because everyone is more focused on the weekend than on the tasks at hand.

Mid-morning and mid-afternoon are the best times to interview

- Best time to interview 9.30a.m.–10.30a.m.
- Worst time to interview 1.00p.m.–2.30p.m.

If possible, you should schedule your interview in the morning, about 9.30a.m. People are usually more alert in the morning and have not had enough time to have a bad day. It is usually after 10.30a.m. when problems and disruptions start. You should not interview before 9.30a.m. because people take a good half hour to get through the morning post and paperwork and to get their bearings. By 9.30a.m., however, the coffee has kicked in and interviewers will be ready for you.

Avoid interviewing near lunch

After 11.00a.m., interviewers will start to get hungry and will be thinking more about lunch than your skills for the job. It is much better to interview earlier in the morning.

The absolute worst time to interview is right after lunch. Typically, after eating, neither you nor the interviewer will be alert, and the interview will not go well.

When I interviewed candidates, I hated that first interview after lunch. Inevitably, I would become sleepy. This always caused me considerable distraction. The person I was interviewing had to be extremely good to make a big impression on me.

After eating, most people need a good hour to fully digest their meal and wake up. If you must interview in the afternoon, try to schedule it between 2.30p.m. and 3.30p.m. After 3.30p.m., interviewers will be thinking more about going home than about your job credentials.

For me, the last interview of the day was always the pits. At that point, my voice was dead and I was tired of asking the same questions over and over again. I have yet to participate in a good interview at the end of the day.

2. What If I Cannot Be The First Person To Interview?

If you are not the first person to be interviewed, the key is to raise the bar so that you stand out from your competition. You can do this by changing the rules of the game. By expanding the role of the position and what you can add to it, you can become the new first impression in the minds of interviewers.

When you raise the bar and redefine what qualities and experiences are necessary for the position, you totally change the playing field. You can now become the new first impression.

3. What Are The Small Things That Make A Big Difference?

In everyday life, it is often the little things that can make or break a situation. Interviewing is no different. The tips that I am going to give you in this section should not be taken lightly.

Avoid eating and drinking during interviews

When interviewing, do not drink, eat or chew gum. Not only is this unprofessional, but it could annoy interviewers. I have actually interviewed people who chewed gum like a cow gnawing on grass. All I could think of was watching their mouths go up and down, up and down. What did they say? Who knows? Who cares? All I wanted to do was get them out of my office.

There may be times when interviewers might offer you a soft drink, coffee or water. What should you do? I recommend that you politely turn down the offer. I say this for two reasons. First, having a beverage gives you one more thing to worry about. You start thinking more about the drink than the interview. Second, a beverage gives you a great target to knock over. If you are like me, and use hand gestures when you speak, you could spill a hot cup of coffee into the interviewer's lap – not a good idea!

Listen, listen and listen

As humans, you were created with two ears and one mouth for a reason. You should listen twice as much as you talk. Quite often, people hear but do not listen. Pay attention and keep good eye contact. If you are well prepared, your mind will not need to wander while the other person is talking. By listening carefully, you will be able to respond more intelligently to statements and questions.

Never interrupt the interviewer

You may be so excited about something that was said that you want to respond before interviewers have a chance to finish with what they have to say. If you do this, interviewers will get upset and eventually switch off. Wait for interviewers to finish their thoughts before talking. I know it can be tough. But remain silent until your interviewers are finished with what they want to say.

More interviewing 'don'ts'

- Don't share proprietary information about your existing employer.
- Don't ramble on. An interviewer's time is valuable. Don't waste it. Make sure that before you say something, you answer in your mind 'So what?' If you were the interviewer, would you care about what you are going to say? If the answer to 'So what?' is positive, then go ahead.
- Don't ever disparage your current company. Be positive in stating why you are leaving; if this is not possible, don't say why you are leaving. Give your current boss and employer high praises. Then, shift the focus to the fact that you are ready for the next challenge. Nobody wants to hire a complainer or a chronic problem.
- Don't tell interviewers what you are currently earning. If you mention how much you are currently making, you have just capped your potential offer. By not mentioning current remuneration, you place yourself in a much better bargaining position.
- Don't show up late to the interview. That will immediately leave a bad taste in the interviewer's mouth. You will probably be rejected just because of that.

More interviewing 'dos'

- Sit down only when offered.
- Cross your legs only if the interviewer does.
- Eat lightly before the interview and at least an hour in advance. You can celebrate with a good meal afterwards.
- Brush your teeth and use mouthwash before the interview. Bring breath mints with you. Keep your breath fresh!
- If you wish, ask if you may take notes.
- After each interview, grade yourself. Ask yourself what you did well on and where you could have improved. Write down notes on these areas so you can improve on your interviewing techniques.
- Smile and have fun!

4. What Can And What Can't Interviewers Ask?

When it comes to interviewing, hopefully you will not have to deal with any legal issues. But no book on job hunting would be complete without giving you an overview of your rights.

I would like to preface what I am about to share with you by saying that I am not a lawyer and much of what I will say can be left up to interpretation. This is for information purposes only and shall not be construed as formal legal advice. To find out exactly what your rights are, you should refer to a lawyer or a governmental agency.

With that disclaimer made, I want to give you an idea of the topics and questions that are off limits to interviewers. In an interview, it is important for interviewers to keep the questions to relevant work-related history. Very personal topics (about age, religion, etc.) have no relevance in an interview. In fact, many of the following topics are illegal to discuss in the interview setting.

Inappropriate interview topics

- Marital status
- Number of children
- Age
- Religion

- Political affiliation
- Health issues
- Sexual orientation
- Trade union membership.

Interviewers are not allowed to ask a man questions they would not ask a woman, or vice versa. In addition, interviewers cannot ask any question of a minority that they would not ask of a non-minority.

Unfortunately, some interviewers have unlawfully used their position for personal gain. You should know what your rights are, especially when it comes to harassment.

For more information

If you want further information on what your rights are, you can contact the Citizens Advice Bureau online (www.adviceguide.org.uk), or contact your local branch (you can find the number from your local telephone directory). Alternatively, try the Commission for Equality and Human Rights (www.equalityhumanrights.com).

Keep the interview focused on 'position-relevant' information

If you are asked questions that you feel are not appropriate, or you are in a situation where harassment is present, my best advice is to politely state that you would like to keep the interview focused on relevant topics and not discuss personal aspects. If the situation gets worse, your best bet is to end the interview. If people like this are managing and working at the company, you will probably not want to work there in any case. Depending on the severity of the situation, you may want to obtain the advice of legal counsel.

You have a right to an open and fair interview, where you are judged on your merits, not on your race, gender, beliefs or other non-relevant personal information.

5. What Is The Best Way To Approach A 'Panel' Or Group Interview?

Sometimes companies will have two or more people interview you at the same time. I'll never forget one interview I had, during my last year at university, with a major appliance manufacturer. They asked me to sit at the head of a boardroom table. No fewer than eight people sat around the table, firing questions at me as if I was a punch bag. At first, I wasn't sure what to do, but I tried to treat each person as if they were the final decision-maker. It worked! I got the job offer.

As it turns out, the best strategy to use is to treat each and every person with equal importance. When you are answering a question, be sure to look at each individual. Just as a teacher tries to make eye contact with every pupil, do the same thing in a group interview.

At the end of the interview, ask the group 'What is the next step in the process for me to become a part of your team?' At that point, they should tell you the person that you should follow up with. Then, after the interview, send each and every person a thank-you note. If they all took the time to participate, it is likely that they all have an input in the decision.

6. How Should I Prepare For A Phone Interview?

The best way to prepare for a phone interview is to put in the same kind of effort and energy that you would for a face-to-face interview. In fact, I even recommend wearing business professional attire. Believe it or not, people can sense how you are dressed, even over the phone. Also, when you are dressed professionally, you will be much more likely to perform at the top of your game.

Follow each of the interview phases we discussed earlier in this book and know your objective before you pick up the phone. Just as with a face-to-face interview, at the end of the phone interview go for the close! In this case, the close will probably be a follow-up interview.

7. Any Suggestions On Interviewing During A Meal?

Interviewing over a meal can be very challenging. It's hard to balance eating and interviewing at the same time. Typically, if an interviewer wants to interview you over a meal, that person wants to foster a more casual environment than that of a stiff office.

When interviewing during a meal, order something that is easy to eat and relatively inexpensive. Stay away from dishes such as pasta and nachos. Always wait for the interviewer to start eating before you do. Don't talk with your mouth full and don't finish the entire course. Unless the interviewer insists, stay away from dessert. You don't want to become tired during your interview by getting a 'sugar crash'.

Try to be a little more casual than you would be in an office environment. Also, try to make your answers a little more concise. If it is a crowded restaurant, it will be difficult to hear. Keep your message as short and to the point as possible. At the end of the interview, thank the interviewer and once again go for the close.

8. What Should I Do When Asked About Remuneration?

At all costs, try to avoid giving a specific expectation figure during the interview. If you provide a figure that is too low or too high, you will lose. And if your figure is in the ballpark, you have just capped what your offer can be.

The best way to approach this topic is to say something like 'I hope to be a top performer for your organisation. As a result, I would like to be remunerated accordingly.' Or you could say something like, 'Based on my track record, I would like to be remunerated at a similar level to other top performers in your company.'

But, whatever you do, try not to give any salary specifics. If they keep trying to nail you down on a specific figure, say to them, 'I am really excited about the opportunity. Please tell me the best offer that you can do and I will do the same.'

9. What Is The Most Common Job-Hunting Mistake?

The most common mistake people make is to just jump into the job hunt without first deciding what they really want to do for a living. Consequently, their focus and messaging is confused and they have a very difficult time finding a job. After all, if you don't know what you want to do, how is anyone else supposed to know?

You will be competing against people who are absolutely passionate about what they want. You need to be able to match that passion in order to succeed. No one can tell you what you want to do for a living. Only you can decide that. Take your time and go for a job you can be passionate about.

10. What Is The Best Way To Handle An Objection?

First, be honest. If the concern is true, acknowledge it. Then, put yourself in your potential employer's shoes. Say to them 'If I were in your shoes I'd be concerned about that too. However, let me show you how I can contribute . . .'.

Then, turn the negative to a positive. 'Granted, I don't have a lot of experience, but you would have to employ two people to give you the same kind of energy and enthusiasm that I will bring to the table.'

Finally, ask 'Did that answer your question or concern?' If not, try again. If so, move on. Two of the most common objections people encounter in interviews are the classics 'you have too little experience' and 'you have too much experience'.

Now I will show you some key selling points and benefits you can focus on to overcome those two most common objections. Regardless of the objection or the concern, there is always a way to turn a negative into a positive.

'Being a recent graduate, you have no experience'
- Will work twice as hard because of my youth and energy
- Learned the latest techniques at university or college
- I can introduce fresh ideas
- Driven to succeed because I have to prove myself
- Too young to have learned bad habits

- You can pay me $^1/_3$ less yet get greater productivity and results
- Being young, it is easier for me to fit into your corporate culture.

'You have too much experience'

- Why invest time and money training someone? I can jump right in
- Being experienced, I'll be twice as productive
- I can make an immediate contribution to your team
- I have a proven track record of success
- I know what it takes to succeed
- You'll gain immediate and measurable results
- With me, you'll get an immediate return on your investment
- Why take a risk on someone with less experience?

Checklist Summary

✓ When possible, try to be the first person to interview
✓ The best times to interview are 9.30a.m. on Tuesdays and Thursdays
✓ Don't forget the small things that make a big difference
✓ Never interrupt interviewers; let them finish their thoughts
✓ Know your legal rights before you go into the interview
✓ When interviewing with a group, treat each person as a decision-maker.
✓ Dress and prepare for phone interviews as for a face-to-face interview
✓ Avoid talking about salary during your interviews
✓ Know what you want – and you will get it
✓ To overcome objections, turn negatives into positives.

'In interviews you should listen twice as much as you talk.'

Recommended Books

Brady, Karren. *Playing to Win: 10 Steps to Achieving Your Goals*. Capstone, 2004.

Brown, Les. *Live Your Dreams*. Avon, 1996.

Buckingham, Marcus and Donald Clifton. *Now, Discover Your Strengths: How to Develop Your Talents and those of the People You Manage*. Free Press, 2002.

Everett, Lesley. *Walking Tall: Key Steps to Total Image Impact*. McGraw-Hill, 2002.

Grabhorn, Lynn. *Excuse Me, Your Life Is Waiting: The Astonishing Power of Feelings*. Hampton Roads Publishing Company, 2003.

Morris, Steve and Graham Willcocks. *Successful CVs in a Week*. Hodder & Stoughton, 1998.

Robbins, Anthony. *Awaken the Giant Within: How to Take Immediate Control of Your Mental, Emotional, Physical & Financial Destiny*. Simon & Schuster, 1992.

Tracy, Brian. *Goals: How to Get Everything You Want – Faster Than You Ever Thought Possible*. Berrett-Koehler Publishing, 2003.

Index